Elgar the Cyclist

A Creative Odyssey

IN WORCESTER & HEREFORD

KEVIN ALLEN

Published in 2005 by Stuart-Clark & Associates cc trading as Publishing Print Matters
34 Balfour Road, Rondebosch 7708, Cape Town, South Africa
www.printmatters.co.za

First published, 1997 by Kevin Allen,
2, Milford Court, Gale Moor Avenue, Alverstoke, Gosport, Hampshire, PO12 2TN

ISBN 0-620-35031-8

Printed and bound by Clyson Printers, 11th Avenue, Maitland 7405, Cape Town, South Africa

Design & Production: Stuart-Clark & Associates cc, Cape Town, South Africa
Formatting: Design Drawer cc, Johannesburg, South Africa

Contents

Introduction & Acknowledgements

List of Illustrations

CHAPTER 1

Birchwood Days: *'Wobble round ...'* – *1*

CHAPTER 2

Malvern Days: *'E. can now go beautifully...'* – *15*

CHAPTER 3

Intermezzo: *'Dorabella'* – *45*

CHAPTER 4

Hereford Days: *'Heavenly country to ride in ...'* – *53*

APPENDIX:

List of Elgar's Destinations – 69

For Daniel,
Cyclist Extraordinary

Introduction

And Acknowledgements

Sometimes sheer petty irritation can be as valuable a spur to action as anything else. This account would probably never have been attempted had I not chanced to see an item on local television news earlier this year, featuring a reporter perched on a mountain bike somewhere high up on the Malvern Hills, exhorting cyclists to 'follow in the tracks of Elgar.' Elsewhere I have heard the claim that 'Elgar was the first mountain biker. 'The television report was something of a misrepresentation of an initiative by the Malvern Tourist Office to encourage cycling in true Elgarian style – around the Hills, not on them; but it is difficult at times to escape the feeling that continued myth-making about Elgar persists in that place above all which should seek to encourage authentic knowledge of his life and work.

Sometimes that local myth-making would seem to be engineered for the crudest of materialistic reasons. 'Elgar's connections with such-and-such an area remain a largely untapped tourism resource,' is the kind of comment that one finds in the local press. Far more blatantly exploitative have been the efforts of Estate Agents and their clients concerning the advertisement of properties with Elgar connections. In the early 1980s, for example, Hazeldine House, the Roberts' former family home at Redmarley, was put on the market. Students of Elgarian biography may be surprised to know that the Agent's prospectus informed potential buyers that the House was built by Major General Sir Henry Roberts, whose only daughter Caroline Alice, 'by local legend eloped with Elgar in 1886 and married him at the Brompton Oratory, London. Later when in October 1886 Edward Elgar opened a studio in Malvern the family were reconciled only shortly before her father died in 1887. To this day the dining room is known as the Reconciliation Room.' Apart from the utter absurdity of the very idea of Alice (how horrified she would be!) – or Edward, for that matter – indulging in an elopement, a little elementary research would have shown that Major General Roberts died in 1860 and the marriage took place in 1889. More recently, the Wells House School at Malvern Wells, where Elgar taught in the 1880s, and now for sale, has featured in the national press as the place where *Land of Hope and Glory* – which in fact appeared some twenty years later – was 'thought' to have been composed.

Elgar himself knew all about Estate Agents. Some house-hunting experiences in London shortly after his marriage led him to write a Longfellow-style poem which concluded:

But I never found the Agents'
Siren-songs one jot fulfillèd ;
Mere delusions, sad & sorry,
Found I ever everywhere –
But I sometimes in my Rambles
Through the foul lanes they had sent me,
Paused by some neglected grave-yard
For awhile to muse & ponder ;
And I thought & whispered softly, –
What a lying lot they are !

Come to that, Elgar had some equally uncomplimentary opinions about Malvern, a town characterised for him by his unhappy hours as a violin teacher in various of its educational establishments, by its rigid Victorian codes of social behaviour, and by its provincial philistinism. 'Oh ! think of Malvern,' he would groan in mock horror while enjoying himself in the freer atmosphere of holidays abroad, and in writing to a friend who was organising a chamber concert in the town he said, 'Do not forget to put Assembly Rooms, Malvern, on the book . . .. It wd. be well to put a special short note saying – "As the Public Hall is engaged the Society has (unfortunately) been obliged to come to that benighted Paradise – MALVERN, etc." – & anything else vitriolic and unpleasing to the inhabitants you can think of.' Elgar's association with Malvern has been made much of in the tourist brochures, but his real estimation of the place fails to find a mention among the myths.

It is difficult to imagine that present-day Malvern would cause him to improve his opinion. The 1997 Malvern Elgar Festival was unable to provide any of his music at all. Recently the powers that be decided against supporting imaginative and important Arts projects such as a residential study centre for English Music, and the creation of a water-colour gallery of national standing. Instead, and clearly against a strong tide of public opinion, approval has been given for the building of a new supermarket in an already congested town centre. The famous gas lamps along the Wells Road, which date back to the 1860s and which must have lighted Elgar's way home on many occasions, were threatened with replacement, until a sudden U-turn after councillors were branded philistines by the national press.

But enough. Far more enjoyable to turn, with Elgar and his bicycle, to the fields and the orchards, to the sequestered country lanes, to the villages with their black-and-white houses, their Churches and pubs, to the quiet river banks with the eternal skies and the Malvern Hills in the background, and the sound of the 'summer wind among the lofty pines'.

Acknowledgements

For permission to reproduce published material I am grateful to the following: The Elgar Will Trust for extracts from letters and other writings of Sir Edward Elgar; Mr Raymond Monk for extracts from the Diary of Lady Elgar, and for help over many other matters stretching back over several years; Mrs Iris Fresson for extracts from *Edward Elgar, The Record of a Friendship*, by Rosa Burley and Frank Carruthers (Barrie & Jenkins, 1972), and Victor Gollancz Limited for passages from *Elgar as I Knew Him*, by W. H. Reed (1973 edition). John Murray Ltd. have been helpful over the use of material from A. C. Benson's Diary, as has Random House UK over the extract from the Greek Anthology. For permission to use the extract from William Saroyan's *The Bicycle Rider in Beverley Hills*, (Faber) I am grateful to Laurence Pollinger Limited and the Stanford University Libraries. I am grateful also for the opportunity to include material from *The Elgar-Atkins Friendship*, by Wulstan Atkins MBE, (David & Charles, 1984) by kind permission of the publishers. I have drawn gratefully on Claud Powell's introduction to his mother's book, *Edward Elgar: Memories of a Variation*, (4th Edition, Scolar Press, 1994), for information concerning her bicycling, and I am indebted to Patricia Egerton-Smith for reminiscences of her Aunt, Isobel Fitton, including the 'rook-roasting' expedition. Vivien Bowkley kindly provided the rare early photograph of Troyte Griffith, originally in possession of the late Rennie Bere, and has given much invaluable help besides, to this and other projects. I am most grateful to Nina Driver for allowing me to make use of the anecdote concerning Elgar at Queenhill Church, told to her mother, Vera Hockman. I regret that at the time of going to press, it has not proved possible despite various efforts, to make contact with Keith Alldritt, who now lives abroad.

For advice and information on cycling history and Lady Harberton, I am grateful to John Pinkerton and Les Bowerman. John Hunt has shared memories of cycling in Worcestershire and Herefordshire in pre-war days, and has offered advice and suggestions. Christopher Bennett of the Elgar Birthplace Museum has advised on many of the illustrations featured in this book, and has organised their reproduction. The kind ladies of Malvern Public Library have efficiently dealt with my many requests for books and documents, and I am grateful to the Worcester and Hereford City Libraries for allowing reproduction of period County maps on the covers of this edition.

I gratefully acknowledge photograph illustrations as follows: front cover images and page 42, Raymond Monk; pages 3, 12, 20, 33, 41 and 64, Elgar Birthplace; page 5, Les Bowerman; page 6, Vivien Bowkley; page 11, Peter Norbury. Pages 24 & 26: Mrs Pam Harber kindly allowed me to photograph the Duke of York at Berrow, and Mr Paul Cowdery generously provided the period photograph of the New Inn, now the Newtown Inn, at Lower Eggleton; I can warmly recommend both establishments! John Pinkerton most kindly helped with copies of pages from his edition, with Derek Roberts, of the Sunbeam Catalogues. The copy of Mr Robbins' advertisement was taken from the Malvern Gazette. Other photographs are from the author's collection.

Before I was sixteen I had many bicycles . . . But the thing about my bicycles that I want to remember is the way I rode them, what I thought while I rode them, and the music that came to me . . .

I rode them with speed and style. I found out a great deal about style from riding them. Style in writing, I mean. Style in everything. I did not ride for pleasure. I rode to get somewhere . . . I mean I rode to get somewhere myself . . .

A bike can be an important appurtenance of an important ritual. Moving the legs evenly and steadily soon brings home to the bike-rider a valuable knowledge of pace and rhythm, and sensible respect for timing and the meeting of a schedule.

Out of rhythm come many things, perhaps all things. The physical action compels action of another order – action of mind, memory, imagination, dream, hope, order and so on. The physical action also establishes a deep respect for grace, seemliness, effectiveness, power with ease, naturalness and so on. The action of the imagination brings home to the bicycle-rider the limitlessness of the potential in all things. He finds out that there are many excellent ways in which to ride a bike effectively, and this acquaintanceship with the ways and the comparing of them gives him an awareness of a parallel potential in all other actions. Out of the action of the imagination comes also music and memory . . .

From *The Bicycle Rider in Beverley Hills*, by William Saroyan.

Illustrations

Elgar cycling on the road between Malvern Wells and Hanley Swan, **front cover**
'A Bicycle of Best Quality' **front & back**
The Wells Road, Malvern **inside front**
'The Royal Sunbeam' detail **title page**
'Nothing Like Outdoor Life' **3**
Lady Harberton **5**
Troyte Griffith and his Brothers **6**
Sherridge **11**
Squire Little **12**
The Post Office at Redmarley **20**
Old Cradley **22**
The *Duke of York* at Berrow **24**
The *New Inn* near Stretton Grandison **26**
The Old Coach Office, Tewkesbury **31**
Longdon Marsh **33**
The Sunbeam Catalogue **37 & 38**
The Elms, Stoke Prior **41**
Elgar and his Father **42**
Ledbury **57**
Eardisland **59**
Interior of Kilpeck Church **64**
Old Brockhampton Manor **66**
Mr. Robbins' advertisement from the Malvern Gazette **inside back**

Birchwood Days

'Wobble round...'

Edward Elgar was by nature an active, outdoor man who was forced by the demands of his work as a composer to spend many hours confined indoors, sitting at his desk writing. Outdoor activity in the beautiful countryside around Malvern and Hereford thus became a welcome change and valuable exercise, as well as a source of inspiration. Elgar was one of the great escapists, and he enjoyed various open-air hobbies over the years, including walking, fishing, horseracing, woodcraft, kite-flying and golf; even playing with a boomerang engaged his attention at one time. But the activity which provided opportunities for an ideal combination of escape, exercise and musical invention was cycling, which he took up for the first time at the age of forty-three, in the summer of 1900.

Cycling had developed rapidly during the eighteen-eighties and nineties. The boneshaker had given way to the velocipede, which gave way to the penny-farthing, which gave way in its turn to the modern-looking safety bicycle, with its chain drive to the rear wheel, diamond frame, pneumatic tyres and more effective brakes. The Midlands became a noted centre of bicycle manufacture, with factories in Coventry, Birmingham and Wolverhampton; and in Worcestershire itself cycle makers set up in Redditch, Kidderminster, Dudley and Bromsgrove, among many other places. An unusual development of local interest was the bicycle of the Danish engineer Mikael Pedersen, who settled in England and worked for many years at the village of Dursley in Gloucestershire – the 'Dursley-Pedersen.' This machine was lightweight and built for speed, being used in various record-breaking rides, and it sported a distinctive woven seat, slung somewhat like a hammock, instead of the usual type of saddle. But there is no evidence that Elgar owned one of these models, for his particular interest in cycling was not in seeing how fast he could go.

Cycling had also become fashionable among the upper and middle classes, and with both men and women. A surprising number of Elgar's friends, including many characters from the *Enigma* Variations, were enthusiastic and experienced cyclists. Among this particular circle was the tall viola-playing Isabel Fitton, whose family lived in Graham Road, Malvern, and who on Midsummer Eve, 1898, undertook a cycling expedition with her younger sister Monica and others to Misummer Hill at the south-west end of the Malverns. In her cycle basket on that occasion, 'Ysobel' was carrying a dead rook, and the planned purpose of the excursion was to roast it at midnight. Monica remembered being disappointed as nothing special happened as the hour approached, and in the event, Isabel graciously declined to roast the poor bird and buried it instead. Another cycling Variation was Winifred Norbury, who lived at a delightful country house, Sherridge, at nearby Leigh Sinton, and who regularly used her bicycle to deliver the Parish magazines round the village and to get to choir rehearsals at Worcester. Sometimes she ventured further, cycling to Hereford for the Opening Service of a Three Choirs Festival on one occasion, and all the way to Ludlow to investigate the famous Castle on another. Equally if not more adventurous was Dora Penny, the daughter of the Rector of Wolverhampton, who several times cycled the forty miles by herself to visit the Elgars. Then there was Arthur Troyte Griffith, the Malvern architect, who would ride over to see the composer at his Hereford home, and George Robertson Sinclair, the organist and owner of the celebrated bulldog Dan, who would drive Elgar to distraction during cycling expeditions by rushing on ahead and hardly waiting for him to catch up. More eccentric still was the somewhat deaf former gold-prospector and cattle-rancher Richard Baxter Townshend, a classical scholar who retired to Oxford and whose own particular machine was a tricycle with a specially adapted bell which rang all the time like an alarm-clock as he cycled past the Colleges. His philosophy was, if he couldn't hear people coming, at least they could hear him, an approach which made sense at a time when the bicycle was thought of as a rather dangerously quiet means of transport. It is easy to hear the wheels going round in his variation, and to imagine him pedalling out of the garden of his house on the Banbury Road, and along through the wide leafy vistas of St. Giles towards Merton College, where he was a member of the Senior Common Room. Other pedalling friends included Ivor Atkins, the Worcester Cathedral Organist, Charles Grindrod the

'Nothing like Outdoor Life'.
Elgar at the gate of Craeg Lea with his second Sunbeam bicycle, with Carice in the background.
From The Sketch, *7 October 1903.*

Malvern doctor, writer and amateur photographer, and Rosa Burley, the charismatic and energetic Headmistress of the Mount School in Malvern, where the Elgars' only daughter, Carice, was one of the pupils.

The cycling *Enigma* ladies showed courage and independence in taking up their hobby. In the days of rigid Victorian codes of dress and public behaviour it had taken a long time for ladies' cycling clothes to become respectable; tight corsets were uncomfortable and restricting while riding, and ankle-length skirts could become entangled with wheels, chain and pedals. Gradually bloomers – baggy pantaloons worn with a knee-length skirt – were introduced from America. Another practical solution, this time from the Continent, was known as Rational Dress, consisting of knickerbockers – long leggings – and a short coat. For a time both alternatives were considered almost indecent and resulted in some wearers becoming the targets of stone-throwing urchins, or being banned from taking refreshments at hotels en route. But many women cyclists bravely stuck with their common-sense clothes and played their part in the gradual emancipation of their sex from domesticity and isolation.

In sleepy Victorian Malvern, where new fashions always came late, it was apparently Florence, Viscountess Harberton, of Oriel House, Tibberton Road, no doubt regarded as something of a local 'character', who introduced a costume of shirt-blouse and bloomers, while fostering the bicycle craze by careering around the district on her ladies' roadster. Earlier, in the 1880s, she had founded the Rational Dress Society at a meeting in Westminster Town Hall chaired by Mrs Oscar Wilde. On that occasion she wore black satin Turkish trousers with a sash, and a waistcoat of white satin and lace with a black velvet jacket. Her ladyship made a fine speech in support of the contention that women should be dressed so that they could take part in sport and games whenever they wanted, emphasizing her points by dramatic cracks of a riding whip. She seemed to have no very high opinion of many of her sisters, for the Rational Dress Society's *Gazette* quoted her as asking:

> *What can be the true state of intelligence of a creature which deliberately loads itself with quantities of useless material round its legs, in spite of discomfort and danger, without any object in view beyond the abject copying of one another? And then, in*

Lady Florence Harberton
From Cycling Magazine *10 May 1911.*

A ladder of Griffith brothers, with Troyte at the bottom; a photograph probably taken sometime in the 1890s at Harrow School, where Griffith senior was a master. Bicycles seem much in evidence.

order to correct the ugliness of such a dress, squeezes in its body until the vital functions can only be carried on imperfectly?

Lady Harberton's concerns may have been provoked by the early death of a daughter from a tubercular condition, exacerbated perhaps by the tight, unhygienic clothing which had become the norm. Later she became something of a suffragist, although there were limits to her radicalism, especially where the privileges of her class were concerned. She was at the centre of a celebrated court case brought by the Cyclists Touring Club on her behalf in 1899, having been relegated to the bar parlour of the Hautboy Hotel at Ockham, Surrey, while wearing rational dress on a cycle outing. The room was smelly, and contained four men, two of whom were actually in working clothes. Her Ladyship retrieved her machine from the stables where she had been forced to hide it, and pedalled off to Cobham where some lunch was eventually found. Rosa Burley herself was influenced by Lady Harberton to take up the cycling craze, but not the bloomers, as she hastened to point out. It would not have done for a Malvern Headmistress, even as independent-minded a one as Miss Burley, to be seen wearing those.

There was no lack of local bicycle dealers to supply the requirements of the growing body of devotees, although some were merely agents whose main business was of an entirely different kind. Henry Jones & Son, for example, were boot and shoe makers of London House, Malvern Link, but they boomed their cycling connection for all it was worth in the *Malvern Gazette* during 1900. 'YOU WANT A BICYCLE?' trumpeted their advertisement, 'get the best, a HUMBER. Lessons in cycling given by Professor Walford. To meet the enormous and ever-increasing demand for a good reliable cycle at a low price, the Makers of the Humber Cycle have decided to devote one of their factories entirely to the production of HIGH GRADE Ladies & Gents cycles at one cost £10. 10. 0d.' Another such agent was J. Harmsher, of St. Ann's Road, Furnishing and General Ironmongers, who referred to their premises as 'THE CENTRAL CYCLE DEPOT,' and boasted of being 'THE OLDEST- ESTABLISHED IN MALVERN.' They offered 'repairs on the shortest notice,' and sold 'Ladies' and Gents' machines with Dunlop Tyres from

£9. 10. 0d.' Their advertisement may have caught Elgar's eye, for they offered also 'Ladies' and Gents' MACHINES for hire by hour, day or week.' A specialist cycle maker seemed to be a certain H. J. Burston, of Newtown Engineering Works, Malvern Link, who produced his very own model, the 'Leader'; his advertisement claimed that the machines were 'selling entirely on their merits' and that they were 'specially built to suit all requirements.' His special boast was apparently that 'Burston's Patent Hollow Joint imparts life and resilience throughout the machine.' Finally and most grandly at this period, the Gazette firmly told its readers to 'Ask for ARTHUR BURGESS, M. E., Practical Cycle and Motor Engineer, Awarded Gold Medal and Diploma for Cycle Construction, Barnard's Green Road.' Mr. Burgess also offered machines for hire, but trounced the competition by offering free lessons and second hand bikes for sale. There was also a private track for racing enthusiasts, and further, 'Repairs, Plating and Enamelling by Practical Men, GUARANTEED.' Those were the days.

It was Rosa Burley who first interested Elgar in cycling. She wrote later that she had often suggested it to him, but he seemed too timid to take it up:

In the summer of 1900 however, I went cycling with some cousins to Scotland where we had a thrilling time which was duly reported to Edward by letter. The result was that when I returned to Malvern I found that he had bought a bicycle which he had been taught to ride by Mr. Little of Birchwood and on which at the first opportunity he wobbled round to the Mount with the suggestion that I should go for a ride with him.

'Wobble round' seems to have been a catch-phrase in Elgar's circle of cycling friends and probably became a standing joke in typical Elgarian style. It was no doubt an accurate enough description of his behaviour as a beginner, for in those days learning to ride a bicycle was thought to be a tricky business. As Miss Burley wrote, Elgar needed lessons, like many people, and his teacher was the active and cheery Henry Little, Squire of the Birchwood Estate at Storridge, to the North-West of the Malvern Hills, and next door to the Norburys. Little was also Elgar's landlord, for the composer rented a small cottage on the then thickly wooded estate, as a quiet working retreat for use

when he could escape from his hated rounds of violin teaching.

That summer of 1900 had seen him working at full stretch for months, composing a work which had to be ready for the Birmingham Festival in early October. The work was *The Dream of Gerontius*, his masterpiece and still today over one hundred years later one of the greatest choral works in the whole repertoire. Within a few years it would be taken up enthusiastically by the great German choirs, and it set Elgar on a path which took him from teaching the violin in Malvern's schools, to world fame, a knighthood, and a unique three-day Covent Garden Festival in his honour. The Elgars would move to bigger houses away from Malvern, firstly at Hereford and then in London, and they would make new friends among wealthy music-lovers who had tired of bicycles and adopted the new craze, that of the motor car. As advancing middle-age took its toll, and as increased fame made money no object, the Elgars would take to hiring a car for the day for drives round the countryside, and the gentler exercise of walking seems to have become preferred to cycling. But all that was in the future that summer as Elgar worked against time to complete the massive orchestral score of *Gerontius* and make sure that the singers and players would have their music in time for rehearsals. Modern technology makes things easier for composers and publishers today, but for Elgar it was an anxious and frustrating time involving endless correspondence and proof-corrections. In the end, as he had feared, the first performance was a poor one, due to lack of proper rehearsal time and the difficulty of the music.

Amid all the hard work and worry at Birchwood Lodge, Rosa Burley's suggestion that he take up cycling must have come as a Godsend to the exhausted composer. It was a perfect safety-valve. We can follow the details from the day-by-day account that Alice Elgar gave of the period in her diary. A bicycle was 'sent for' – presumably hired from one of the obliging gentlemen at Malvern Link – on 10th July, and the necessary lessons with Squire Little began that very day. His method was presumably the standard one at the time; he secured a strong strap round Elgar's waist, held on to it, and ran alongside as he began to 'wobble round.' Elgar had complete faith and confidence in his teacher – 'Squire Little never let me down once, bless him!' he wrote later, and Alice praised his 'unwearied patience.' The process continued for several days, and the roads around Birchwood may not have helped, as they were probably nothing more than bumpy tracks at that time.

If learning to ride a modern-style bicycle might seem hard enough, it could not have been as bad as coping with one of the earlier high-wheel or penny-farthing machines. Mark Twain wrote an account of his first solo venture on such a bicycle, after no less than eight days of tuition. The essay was called *Taming the Bicycle*, and parts of it would I feel sure have appealed to Elgar's sense of humour:

Mine was not a full-grown bicycle, but only a colt – a fifty-inch, with the pedals shortened up to forty-eight – and skittish, like any other colt . . . Of course I had trouble mounting the machine, entirely on my own responsibility, with no encouraging moral support from the outside, no sympathetic instructor to say, "Good! Now you're doing well – good again – don't hurry – there, now, you're all right – brace up, go ahead."In place of this I had some other support. This was a boy, who was perched on a gate-post munching a hunk of maple sugar. He was full of interest and comment. The first time I failed and went down he said that if he was me he would dress up in pillows, that's what he would do. The next time I went down he advised me to learn to ride a tricycle first. The third time I collapsed he said he didn't believe I could stay on a horse-car. But next time I succeeded, and got clumsily under way in a weaving, tottering, uncertain fashion, and occupying pretty much all of the street. My slow and lumbering gait filled the boy to the chin with scorn, and he sung out, "My, but don't he rip along!" Then he got down from his post and loafed along the sidewalk, still observing and occasionally commenting. Presently he dropped into my wake and followed along behind. A little girl passed by, balancing a wash-board on her head, and giggled, and seemed about to make a remark, but the boy said, rebukingly, "Let him alone, he's going to a funeral."

But Elgar's lessons were evidently a great success, and he was pleased with his progress. The day after his first lesson he wrote to his close friend August Jaeger, the subject of the *Nimrod* Variation and Publishing Office Manager at Novello's, emphasizing his preference for books and the outdoor life over the labours of composing:

I was at a book sale yesterday & have a ton to look over – felling one tree in view –

Sherridge, *the 'eighteenth-century house' which 'really suggested' the Eighth Variation according to Elgar, who several times cycled here to visit the Norburys. A more sedate four-wheeled vehicle is in evidence on this occasion.*

Harry Brace Little, Squire of the Birchwood Estate and Elgar's cycling teacher.

blasting another & learning to Bicycle & fifty 1000 nice things to do & all the time I have to be writing new bars to please an old duffer.

Elgar mixed continued lessons with *Gerontius* orchestration, and another machine was sent for so that Alice also could take lessons. By the twenty-third of the month she felt that her husband had succeeded well enough to announce to her diary that he definitely 'could cycle,' and he celebrated the event by riding the very short distance to Birchwood House, Squire Little's home, no doubt 'wobbling round' to thank his teacher and show off his prowess. It was an auspicious day, for it marked the beginning of what must have been several thousands of miles of cycling over the next eight or nine years, exploring a vast area of countryside with the Malvern Hills as a permanent backdrop. Setting off from his house, Craeg Lea, at Malvern Wells, or from Birchwood Lodge, he would reach, among many other places, Kempsey, Spetchley, Worcester and Stoke to the North; Newent, Redmarley, Hasfield and Ross to the South; Longdon, Evesham, Pershore, Tewkesbury and Bredon to the East; and Colwall, Cradley, Ledbury and Hereford to the West. The move to Hereford in 1904 brought a whole new area to be explored, including villages and places with delightful old-fashioned names such as Cleobury Mortimer, Lugwardine, Hampton Bishop, Eardisley, Weston Beggard, Stretton Grandison and one in particular which amused Elgar, Little Dewchurch.

But those miles of cycling did not just represent sight-seeing and exercise. Elgar had always done his composing in the open air, the writing down of it later being almost a mechanical process. Now with cycling to take him further around his favourite countryside than he had ever been before, the new hobby became an indispensable aid and stimulus to his musical thought-processes, for the whole human system, mental and emotional as well as physical, is activated through the bodily chemistry of exercise. Endorphins released into the bloodstream trigger feelings of euphoria, while other chemicals have the effect of improving and extending concentration. So ideal conditions for creative thinking could be established, and it can be no coincidence that Elgar's years of cycling were the years that saw the planning or completion of many of his greatest works – *The Apostles* and *The Kingdom*, the *Introduction and Allegro for Strings*, four of the *Pomp & Circumstance Marches*, the *Wand of Youth* Suites, the First Symphony and the Violin Concerto.

Many people have described Elgar as the 'quintessentially English' composer, and when pressed for a reason have not found it easy to provide one. But it is not difficult to feel the English countryside in his music, as Elgar absorbed it into his mind during hour after hour of steady rhythmic pedalling along quiet lanes. Repeated undulating patterns of fields and hedgerows seem to be echoed in the subtly merging patterns of his music, and the rolling contours of the Malvern Hills are echoed in a favourite habit of developing tunes by the process of repeating sequences. Riding round a wide area, seeing those unchanging Hills from a variety of points of the compass, would be like developing variations on a single theme, or repeating it among different instruments. The behaviour of the weather is also always to the front of the cyclist's mind. A cyclist is particularly vulnerable to changes in the weather, and it is a factor which controls whether he or she can venture out at all. Several times Elgar had to abandon rides due to heavy rain. So the weather is also to be found in his music, and we can hear moments when clouds suddenly darken a clear sky, when the wind sighs through the trees, when thunder growls and explodes, or when the sun breaks gloriously through.

The link in Elgar's mind between music and the natural world around him stood out strongly in a controversial lecture he gave at Birmingham in 1905, which he called 'A Future for English Music.' He wanted to see a new generation of composers, and told them to draw their inspiration from their own country, their own literature, 'and, in spite of what many would say – from their own climate.' He went on to say, 'There are many possible futures. But the one I want to see coming into being is something that shall grow out of our own soil, something broad, noble, chivalrous, healthy and above all, an out-of-door sort of spirit.'

The humble bicycle has brought convenience, economy, exercise, delight and adventure to generations of people since its early days, and now is taking on a new role in encouraging healthier lifestyles and developing clean transport. Its place in English social history is well established. But we tend to forget its role in the creative life of a great composer, and its stimulus towards the creation of some of this country's greatest music through its easy access of that essential 'out-of-door sort of spirit.'

Malvern Days

'E. CAN NOW GO BEAUTIFULLY...'

... was how Alice Elgar described her husband's progress in a letter written on the day in early August 1900, on which he wrote the last notes of the *Gerontius* score. There was much work still to do in correcting and proof-reading, but before long the fate of the work was entirely out of his hands, and all he could do was wait – for two long months. While the weather lasted, cycling was to fill that gap as nothing else could, and as his confidence increased Elgar's rides became longer and longer. By the end of his first season he would have made it as far as Hereford in one direction, and Hasfield, on the way to Gloucester, in the other, and he would have been able also to explore nearer places such as Broadwas, Suckley, Rhydd and Hanley.

But there were still some teething troubles. The very next day after Alice's proud letter, both Elgars pedalled off to see the Norburys at nearby Sherridge House. They ended up having to take turns on Alice's machine as Edward had his first experience of the cyclist's occupational hazard, a puncture. Tandem machines were well established by this time but Edward and Alice seem never to have contemplated a bicycle 'made for two.' Rosa Burley thought that Alice's machine was in fact a tricycle, which presumably she felt safer with. Tricycles were also somehow a little more dignified. Conan Doyle, another cycling fan whose outings stimulated creative ideas – Sherlock Holmes, after all, was familiar with no less than forty two different impressions left by bicycle tyres – and who shared a military-looking appearance with Elgar, had solved the problem by acquiring a tandem tricycle. Such a machine was probably reasonably easy to deal with on the roads around South Norwood, where he lived. But country roads in those days were often shockingly bad: dusty, potholed and stony in summer, muddy and rut-filled in winter. Asphalting did not become common until well into the early years of the century and the increasing advent of the motor-car, and then often only on major roads.

Steam-rollers were a rarity and thorns clipped from hedges, broken glass, and nails which had worked loose from horses' hooves littered the surfaces to plague the unfortunate cyclist. The compensation was in the peace and quiet of almost empty roads, where a man might pedal for miles and dream his dreams without distraction.

Nothing daunted by the puncture, Elgar went to the shop in Malvern Link, from where he had merely hired machines so far, and ordered a model to buy. It was a fortnight in coming, and meanwhile he asked for some repairs to the bicycle he had been using. He was having some tooth trouble at the time, and I wonder if the repairs he asked for were as a result of his own adjustments, for Elgar loved gadgetry. It would fit in nicely with a story he told his good friend and biographer Billy Reed many years later:

> *. . . about a device he had fitted to lock the front wheel so that the machine would stay leaning against a tree or wall in safety, the wheel being rigid instead of wobbling about. He had been a little troubled with toothache, and one day, while writing in his music-room at home, the tooth was worrying him all the time . . . putting down his pen in desperation, he decided that he would proceed at once to the nearest dentist and have the wretched tooth out. With his usual precipitation he rushed out, snatched the bicycle from the wall, and mounted it. A violent header over the handle-bars reminded him that he had forgotten the so-called safety-catch that locked the front wheel.*

In signing off a letter to Jaeger about this time, Elgar seemed to refer to the incident, and threw in another factor that he was to enjoy on cycling jaunts – cider: 'Yours ever with a bad tooth & a shaky hand from Bike riding (falling off I mean) & refreshments.' Perhaps despite all Squire Little's tuition, it was still not quite time to hang up the 'L' plates. Another unfortunate incident was related by Rosa Burley, to whom Elgar had showed off his bicycle as soon as she returned from that tour of Scotland at the end of August. An unexpected encounter with Malvern's aristocratic female pioneer of bicycling seems to have had an unsettling effect on the composer:

> *Our first afternoon out was not a success, for encountering Lady Harberton in Abbey*

Road, he was so overwhelmed that he described a few elaborate flourishes and collapsed with a tinny crash.

Perhaps it was the bloomers. To this day I can never walk past some of those spacious and imposing Victorian houses in Abbey Road without seeing in my mind's eye the composer of *The Dream of Gerontius* collapsing on to the road in front of them, and hearing that 'tinny crash.' Neither was it the last time that such an indignity would be suffered, although it may have been forgivable on this occasion. It seems to have been Elgar's first outing on the new machine, which he collected on 29th August 1900. He would use it for some two and a half years, and as he later told Jaeger, it was a Royal Sunbeam, fixed wheel, 27 inch frame model with a front plunger brake and a Bowden (caliper) rim brake for the rear wheel. The Sunbeam Catalogue for that year shows that it would have had 28 inch wheels, a hand-polished black enamel finish – other colours were available by request – rubber pedals, and an oil-bath in the chain guard, one of the machine's special features. It may have prevented any irritating rattling noise and thus played its own small part in helping the Elgarian concentration on higher things. The Royal Sunbeam was a quality machine, considered an aristocrat among bicycles, first produced by the successful Wolverhampton firm of John Marston Ltd. in 1896. Its cost, according to the firm's 1900 Catalogue, would have been twenty-one pounds, ten shillings. He might have acquired an adequate machine for half the price, but whenever he could, Elgar seems to have worked on the basis that only the best was good enough. When we remember that Novello's initially offered the sum of just two hundred pounds for the rights to *The Dream of Gerontius*, we can see the extent of his commitment to cycling from another angle.

Elgar nicknamed the bicycle 'Mr. Phoebus', partly in a punning reference to the Sunbeam make, for Phoebus was a poetic name for the sun, and partly perhaps after a character in Disraeli's novel, *Lothair*; possibly it was one of what he described to Jaeger as the 'ton' of books he had to 'look over' from the book sale. Both Elgars were wide readers and this novel of Catholic intrigue in high society might have appealed to them. Disraeli's Mr. Phoebus, a minor character in the story, is a successful artist, brilliant and brave, 'accomplished in the daring and graceful pursuits of man.' He has a strong sense of the beautiful, and is a worshipper of nature, believing that men should live in the open air and cultivate strength and suppleness. There were some less healthy eccentricities to his character, but on many grounds the choice of Mr. Phoebus as an identity for the new bicycle seems an appropriate and prophetic one. Elgar must have sensed that once out and about in the saddle, there would be 'music in the air.'

Mr. Phoebus's went back to the shop after a fortnight for routine adjustments, but by this point in time, half way through September, the weather and other events would conspire to restrict Elgar to just two or three more outings that year. He had to be away from home a good deal. There were the London rehearsals of *Gerontius* to attend, and the première itself in Birmingham at the beginning of October, while November saw him travelling by train to Cambridge to receive an honorary degree. The performance of *Gerontius* was very poor and Elgar was upset and disappointed, but many people were not put off by the performance itself and realised that underneath it lay the work of a genius – and the Cambridge degree confirmed it. Together with the *Enigma* Variations of the year before, the new work set him well and truly on the road to international celebrity. That winter, with Mr. Phoebus no doubt properly oiled and stowed away in the garden shed at Craeg Lea, he composed the boisterous *Cockaigne* (In London Town) Overture. It was a complete change of musical mood and style from *Gerontius*, and in composing it Elgar's mind seemed to have travelled from the quiet Worcestershire lanes to the streets of the capital itself. One day he would cycle those as well.

The beginning of the new cycling season saw Elgar firmly back in the saddle in those country lanes. His first ride of 1901 was on 14 March, a short distance through Hanley, with its scattering of black-and-white buildings, to Upton-on-Severn. Ten days later, the *Cockaigne* Overture was finished and cycling gradually began in earnest, with trips to Bosbury, Hawkhurst and Colwall, a village nestling under the western slopes of the Malverns with dramatic views of the Herefordshire Beacon, known as the 'British Camp,' where legend had placed the last stand of the Briton King Caractacus against the Romans. Alice seems never to have taken up cycling as seriously as her husband, but at this time and for some years to come ever-ready cycling companions were to be found in Miss Burley and various members of her family, who ran The Mount School as a joint venture until it eventually had to close due to outbreaks of food poisoning. Some people thought that the unfortunate outbreaks were not unconnected with the activities of Mrs Burley senior in the kitchen, although that may have been unkind. But Rosa Burley seemed to be able to find frequent opportunities to leave her own duties to go cycling with Elgar. There's no point in being a Headmistress if you can't play truant occasionally, after all, and she was always able to give encouragement and understanding to her occasionally moody fellow-cyclist. Like him, too, she was interested in the many historic village churches and other buildings that they came across on their travels. Such joint expeditions between a single lady and an older married man also showed the role that the bicycle might play in challenging the restraints of Victorian convention. Miss Burley remembered how the exercise of cycling did Elgar good that spring and how it brought him in touch with the country scenery and the natural world:

> *There is, perhaps, nothing like physical exercise to dissolve one's worries and our exploration of the three counties of Worcester, Hereford and Gloucester not only took him away for a time, at any rate, from the tiresome problems of his work but brought him in touch with a larger stretch of countryside which he loved and in which he had always found inspiration.*
>
> *Sometimes we would talk, sometimes we would pedal in silence. He was very difficult and one never quite knew what would be the mood of the afternoon. There were times when he was gay and hopeful especially at the beginning of the cycling season when the fresh green on the trees seemed an invitation to take longer and longer rides and he was thankful for release from the winter confinement indoors. I found that he was particularly touched by birdsong and that he loved and knew all the little creatures that darted in and out of the hedges.*

One of the 'difficult' days was 15 April 1901, when Elgar went cycling with Miss Burley and some neighbours. Alice's diary merely tells us, 'E., E. Wilson, E. Griffith & Miss Burley started to bicycle. E returned. Stormy day.' Stormy indeed, as Miss Burley explained:

The Post Office, Redmarley.
(Period postcard photograph)

On one occasion we had taken with us as an addition to the party two neighbours whose conversation irritated him and to make matters worse, a drizzle of rain overtook us. 'Oh, I can't stand this,' Edward suddenly claimed in exasperation. 'Let' s go home!' And without waiting for us he turned back. We paid no attention to him and continued our ride. Relations with him were a bit strained after that.

But all was put right and two days later the foursome were out cycling together again, putting the machines on the train as far as Ledbury with its timbered Market Hall, and then riding westwards to Ross and Newent, and not arriving home that evening until nine o'clock, greatly to the relief of an anxious Alice. If she had been worried by the thought of her husband cycling in the dark, she might perhaps have been reassured by the thought of the gas lamps along the Wells Road, with their gentle glow. Many of them are still functioning, and to this day there is a beautifully preserved Victorian gas lamp opposite Craeg Lea. Later that month Elgar began an occasional habit of riding along that road on Sundays, to attend Mass at St. Wulstan's Roman Catholic Church, Little Malvern; Alice and Carice seem to have walked. Today of course the Churchyard is the last resting place of all three.

Later that April, on the 23rd, Elgar undertook another long ride in the Gloucester direction through Pendock and on to have tea with Alice's old friends, the Bakers, at Hasfield Court, returning through Newent – a lovely hot day, as the diary notes. Next month he found Cradley, Castlemorton, and the picturesque Broadwas, with its church standing by the river's edge. Like so many of the villages that Elgar found, it went back to Domesday and beyond. But then cycling was disrupted as he went to London to make arrangements for the ailing August Jaeger to visit a Harley Street specialist, subsequently inviting him back to Malvern for some country air. Then there was a visit to Wales, followed by the London première of *Cockaigne* on 20 June. Elgar managed only one ride that month, to Worcester via Upton; he returned 'very tired,' Alice noted, and Elgar seems to have felt poorly at this time. He was having to work hard orchestrating his friend Herbert Brewer's work *Emmaus* for the Three Choirs Festival that autumn, and putting together the first two *Pomp & Circumstance* Marches.

Most of Elgar's cycling that year of 1901 was done during July, with eleven outings

Old Cradley, near Malvern.
(Period postcard photograph)

noted in Alice's diary, including tours to Birchwood, Fernshill, Bromyard, Much Cowarne, Clifton-on-Teme, (a village standing high above a favourite river) Cradley again and Ridgway. Squire Little was a companion on one occasion, and so sometimes were the Wilsons, the Craeg Lea neighbours, but Rosa Burley continued to be a regular partner, and particularly remembered seeing Ragged Stone Hill at the southern end of the Malvern range, on one outing. There was a legend that death or disaster would attend anyone who fell under the shadow of this hill, and indeed Dr. Grindrod himself had written a novel based on it. Miss Burley was becoming aware of how Elgar was finding musical inspiration through the rides. The chemistry was beginning to work:

> *There cannot have been a lane within twenty miles of Malvern that we did not ultimately find. We cycled to Upton, to Tewkesbury, to Hereford, to the Vale of Evesham, to Birtsmorton where Cardinal Wolsey is said to have fallen asleep and come under the fatal shadow of the Ragged Stone, to the lovely villages on the west side of the Hills – everywhere. Much of Edward's music is closely connected with the places we visited for, as we rode, he would often become silent and I knew that some melody, or, more probably, some new piece of orchestral texture, had occurred to him. Unlike most composers he carried no notebooks in those days but seemed able to register and remember his musical ideas even in the middle of a conversation.*

There was an outing early in August, when Elgar made it to Hereford again before getting down to the *Pomp & Circumstance* Marches in earnest. Another break in Wales was followed by the Three Choirs Festival at Gloucester. One final ride with Miss Burley took place that autumn, before the première of the Marches during October. They were an immediate sensation, and the trio tune from the first would gain immortality as 'Land of Hope and Glory.' Elgar later told King Edward that the tune had come to him while fishing, but is it not possible to feel the rhythm of steady pedalling behind the regular tread of its accompaniment?

The increasing demands of fame kept Elgar busy that winter. In December there was a performance of *Gerontius* in Dusseldorf, and the composer and his wife spent Christmas

The Duke of York, *at Berrow, where Elgar and Dr Grindrod took shelter during a storm on 9 May 1903. Eventually they were obliged to put themselves and their bicycles on a passing baker's cart.*

there. The New Year saw the Funeral March from *Grania & Diarmid* played in London, and in the spring there were further performances of the Marches and *Cockaigne*. It was a fitting prelude to an important year in Elgar's life, for he had received the special compliment of being asked to provide a *Coronation Ode*, setting verses by the celebrated writer and diarist A. C. Benson, to celebrate the accession of the new King, Edward VII. It was a sign that he was already seen as virtually the country's leading composer, and people must have thought that the commission would be bound to be rewarded at some stage with an honour. But the Elgars kept such thoughts to themselves. On 5 March, 1902, Alice marked the beginning of the new cycling season: 'E. rode Mr. Phoebus 1st time this year, Hanley, &c.'

Next day he was out with Miss Burley and they took tea at the *Duke of York*, just off the main Gloucester road at Berrow. The event was celebrated with a card to Ivor Atkins, the cycling Worcester Cathedral organist, saying 'biking's begun,' together with a musical doodle. Work on the Ode left him time for just short rides, to such familiar places as Hanley, Upton, Pershore and Cradley, whose Church contained a nine-foot parish chest with five locks, said to be cut out of a single tree trunk. Much of the *Coronation Ode* was sent off to the publishers on 26 March, and Elgar replied that day to Ivor Atkins concerning a proposal to meet up at Colwall on their bicycles. If Elgar were busy, Atkins had suggested, it would save time if he were to walk Mr. Phoebus there over the Hill. The idea did not find favour, and the reply seems to show that Elgar never considered cycling on the Hill itself:

> *Your Friday scheme is noble but no good bikily: Look 'ere! If I walk to Colwall pushing the Bike over the hill I shall get 1/4 mile ride – & have to push the Bike all the way back here.*

I wonder if Elgar knew of the achievement of the noted Malvern cyclist Frank Walford, who in 1893 wheeled his bicycle to the top of the Worcestershire Beacon, mounted, and proceeded to descend. The cycling Press reported, 'The prospect from the summit is enough to daunt the heart of the stoutest rider . . . the witnesses vainly endeavoured to persuade him from the attempt, but, nothing daunted, he bade them farewell, and with his hand firmly grasping the brake commenced, and successfully

The New Inn, *the 'little roadside pub' near Stretton Grandison which Elgar and Rosa Burley visited on 24 June 1902, and where they first heard the news of the cancellation of the Coronation of Edward V11.*

accomplished this most daring and remarkable feat.' Walford was the 'Professor' of Henry Jones & Son's Cycle Agency in Malvern Link.

Elgar went out just twice in April, once with Miss Burley to Dunstall Castle, noted by Pevsner as a 'sham Norman castle ruin,' at Earl's Croome near Upton. The *Coronation Ode* began to claim most of his time, and life was getting very busy. In May there was another Dusseldorf *Gerontius*, and Elgar returned from Germany in early June to travel more or less straight on to Sheffield, and then London, for *Ode* rehearsals. The London practices included the forty-piece Military Band that was to be used with such overwhelming effect in the final number, 'Land of Hope and Glory,' included by special request of the King. Once again Elgar's work was largely done and there was now some spare time for cycling before the Coronation itself on 26 June. The gap was to provide opportunity for a very strange incident that Elgar remembered all his life. On the 21st he set out from Craeg Lea by himself eastwards through the Severn Valley:

> *E out early rode to Bredon, Kemerton, sought for Mr Allen's grave found the stone had fallen down the night before.*

Elgar himself told the full story many years later to his first major biographer, Basil Maine, with a 'naive touch of mystery and awe':

> *Allen, it will be remembered, was the solicitor in whose office Elgar had worked as a boy. One day, about fifteen years after he had left the office, Elgar was cycling in the country near Worcester. At a cross-roads he was intending to turn to the left but was surprised by the sudden appearance of a cart load of hay drawn by three horses, and was compelled to take the right hand turning. Farther on, he arrived at another cross-roads and was about to take the left-hand turning when another cart-load of hay, again drawn by three horses, forced him to the right. He cycled on and slowly began to realise he was on the road that led to the village where Allen was buried. Then it was that he resolved to visit the grave. He arrived at the grave-yard and found there the sexton's wife. "Can you help me find the grave of William Allen?" he asked. For a moment, the woman, with a scared look on her face, stood dumb and still. Then she said, "Funny you should be askin'. Why the stone o' that grave fell down and broke*

this very morning. We were wonderin' if there were any relations or friends we could write to about it."

Something else on a much more practical level struck Elgar at this time, and next day he wrote to Dora Penny about his tyres, 'I have had my tyres going on into their 3rd season: 1300 miles. Ought I to buy new ones or will these last without busting for a few months?' History records nothing about any new tyres, but before too much longer Elgar would dispense with his fixed wheel machine and enjoy the easier ride of a free wheel. That same day, he wrote to Jaeger in London mocking the friends who would not go cycling with him, and revealing his delight in the 'ploughman's lunch.' He was not looking forward to the time he would have to spend in London for the Coronation festivities:

I hate coming to town – shall miss the haymaking I fear. Had 50 miles ride yesterday amongst the Avon country – Shakespeare &c &c. Oh ! so lovely but solus 'cos I can't find anybody here foolheaded enough to eat bread & cheese & drink beer – they've all got livers & apparently live in the country 'cos they can't afford to be swells in a town.

Elgar was determined to make the most of his cycling interlude, and was out early again the next day, riding to Berrow and Redmarley, the Gloucestershire village where Alice's family had lived at Hazeldine House. One more day was all he had after that, and he used it to ride with Rosa Burley as far as Stretton Grandison. She remembered it well:

On 24 June, two days before the Coronation, we visited Stretton Grandison, a village just off the old Worcester-Hereford main road, where there is a fine Church. It had been a hot day and after our usual examination of the church we managed to get some tea at the inn. This ride was to mark the end of our outings for the time being as on the next day Edward and Alice were to go up to town for the festivities.

Edward was already very full of this affair, the importance of this occasion and of the Court Dress he was to wear, while conducting the Ode. On an impulse I said as we ate our simple tea, 'Does it strike you that the King is going to have an extremely trying time these next few days?'

Edward agreed that to attend a gala performance immediately after reviewing the fleet at Spithead – a trying affair indeed with the glare of the sun and the booming of the guns – followed by a train journey, might prove a strain to one who, like the King, was known not to be strong.

'I think you'll find that he'll do it, though,' he said.

A few minutes later the innkeeper's wife burst in upon us with the news that the King had been taken seriously ill and that the Coronation, and, in consequence, all the celebration, had been postponed sine die.

It was a terrible disappointment for Edward who once again had to face the shattering of bright hopes, and he returned home in gloomy anticipation of the blow which must of necessity fall on poor Alice. She was in fact the worse sufferer of the two as she had no satisfactory outlet for her misery, whereas Edward found consolation in action. During the next few days we covered an enormous distance on our bicycles.

And in another account Miss Burley wrote that Elgar remained very calm, and said, 'Well, I shall have a few days bicycling that's all.' He went out cycling every day for the next four days, in fact, reaching Clifton-on-Teme again and finding Shelsey Walsh, whose church of St. Andrew has a timber bell-turret and a Norman nave. With his romantic love of history and local lore, Elgar probably knew of Sir Richard, the last of the Walsh line, who was High Sheriff of Worcestershire at the time of the Gunpowder Plot, and who helped to capture the schemers at Holbeach House. Jaeger wrote to commiserate over the *Coronation Ode* débâcle, but Elgar replied:

Don't, for heaven's sake, sympathise with me – I don't care a tinker's damn! It gives me three blessed sunny days in my own country (for which I thank God or the devil) instead of stewing in town. I was biking out in Herefordshire yesterday & the news reached me at a little roadside pub: I said 'Give me another pint of cider.' I'm deadly sorry for the King – but that's all.

During the first half of July the outings continued and hardly a day passed without

Elgar getting out on his bicycle, usually to familiar destinations like Redmarley, Broadwas, Worcester or Hereford; but a new destination appears in the diary on the 2nd – Longdon Marsh near Upton, where Elgar saw a heron fishing. It was a tidal marsh until drainage and still floods in winter. The flat, desolate area, haunted by rows of willows, came to hold a fascination for Elgar, and he would go there more and more frequently to find musical inspiration. The cycling therapy, together with music, seemed to be doing the trick in helping Elgar to get over the disappointment of the cancelled Coronation. He wrote to Jaeger, 'I have been biking wildly – but not too well – during the last 10 days & playing Bach, who heals and pacifies all men & all things.'

He pedalled again to Hereford to stay with the organist Sinclair, and as a result wrote to Atkins, 'I've been tasting cider & have a head!' He rode back to Malvern a couple of days later, and Alice found him poorly from too much sun while riding; perhaps she didn't know about the cider. But he recovered in time to go to Germany for the Bayreuth Festival, and on his return began to think seriously about his next major choral work, *The Apostles*, for the Birmingham Festival of October, 1903. It may have seemed a long time away, but Elgar did not have a ready-made text as he had for *Gerontius*, and much time had to be spent in choosing and combining passages from different parts of the Bible. The whole process of assembling the words and composing the music over the next year or so became a massive, nerve-racking task, requiring many inspirational bike-rides. But the crisis over that work was still to come, and during August Elgar made the first of several longer and more ambitious rides when he cycled back to Malvern after staying with a friend who lived near Chester. He put up overnight at Shrewsbury, and put Mr. Phoebus on the train between Ludlow and Hereford, but it was a fair challenge for a forty-six year old and Alice was most relieved to see him arrive home; she 'began to be frightened but he came safe.' September saw the Three Choirs Festival, and some more local rides, but another more lengthy run was attempted when Elgar spent a few days in London for more rehearsals of the *Coronation Ode*, which received its delayed first performance at Sheffield in early October. He hired a machine and cycled to his friends the Speyers who lived at a house called Ridgehurst at Shenley in Hertfordshire, a distance of some seventeen miles. It seems to have been his last outing of 1902, and was not without incident, as he explained apologetically to Jaeger. 'I am so sorry I

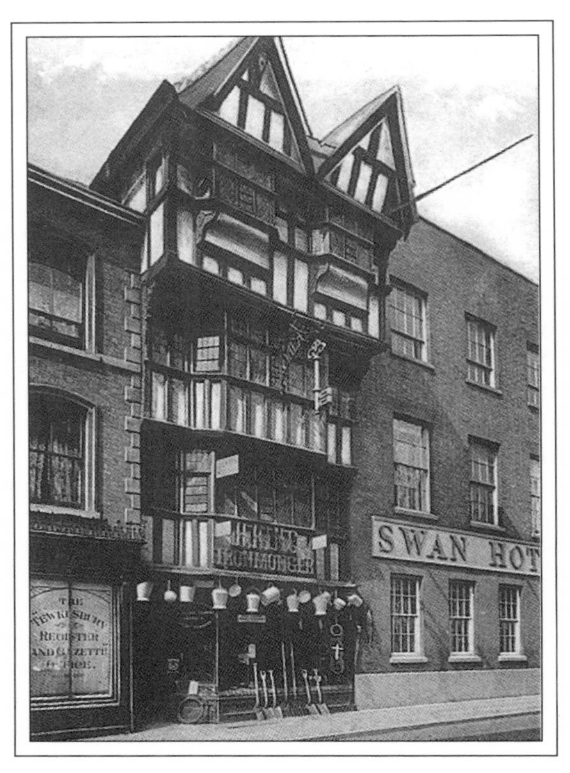

The Old Coach Office, Tewkesbury.
(Period postcard photograph)

saw so little of you in London,' he wrote, 'I rode (bike) to Ridgehurst on Saturday after the St. James's Hall rehearsal & knocked a Man off en route.'

Cycling through the crowded streets of central London must have been a different proposition from quiet country lanes, and accidents were bound to happen with so much horse transport still around, motor traffic on the increase, and lane discipline unknown. People seemed to walk into the roads with complete unconcern, and bicycles were deceptively silent. Some years earlier, even such an exalted figure as Lord Randolph Churchill had asked anxious questions in the House about pneumatic-tyred bicycles which 'come silently and stealthily upon one.'

Elgar's main creative preoccupation that winter and for most of 1903 was *The Apostles*, and work went slowly and painfully at first. His first ride of the new year was unusually early, and was clearly connected with the problems experienced with the composition of the new work. Alice Elgar's diary for 30 January, 1903, reads, 'E. worried over Apostles. E tried a little bicycling and rode 16 miles.'

The next day she described him as working at composition 'but not too happily.' The winter did not help. '. . . the weather is too cold for me to go and sit in the marsh with my beloved wild creatures to get heartened up and general inspiration,' Elgar told Jaeger. But with some improvement in the temperature, cycling again came to the rescue, this time with a fresh impetus as Elgar discovered the advantages of the free-wheel over the fixed. Early in February he hired a free-wheel machine and took it for a sixteen mile run, and three days later, on the day he finished the first scene of the new work, he ordered such a model, apparently from another, newer, local shop whose advertisements began to appear in the Malvern Gazette that year. A Mr. A. H. Robbins, of Colston Buildings, Malvern Link ('The Noted House for Travelling Trunks') advised that he was the 'Sole Agent for the Noted SUNBEAM CYCLES,' and so it would seem that Elgar remained loyal to the Sunbeam make. Mr. Robbins also sold puncture repair outfits at 6d, 8d or 1/-, new inner tubes at 4/6, and lamps for 1/9d. The new machine took nearly a month to arrive, and meanwhile Elgar seems to have confined himself to short rides to places such as Ham Court and Eastington, with its splendid timber-framed

Longdon Marsh, a photograph taken by the late Alan Webb in the 1930s.

Hall, in one direction, and Sherridge at Leigh Sinton in the other. Perhaps it was Elgar who told his friend Troyte Griffith, a talented painter as well as an architect, about Eastington Hall, resulting in a water-colour painting which brings out all the sixteenth-century charm of the building. He found a new cycling companion at this time in Dr. Charles Grindrod, who was a distinguished amateur photographer in addition to his medical and literary interests. Grindrod lived at the Wyche cutting, near to Craeg Lea, and Elgar sat for a portrait photograph on 9 February. 'E & Grindrod go for ride after photo,' wrote Alice, and the photo turned out to be one of the great images of Elgar the dreamer, a classic of its kind.

While waiting for the new free-wheel bicycle, Elgar wondered how best to dispose of Mr Phoebus. He decided to offer that gentleman to August Jaeger, whose health had been poor for a long time with a series of nose and throat problems. Eventually he would die of tuberculosis in middle age, and living in heavily polluted London must have hastened the progress of his illness. Around this time he had moved house from low-lying West Kensington to Muswell Hill in north London, with its fresher air and open spaces, and Elgar saw the opportunity to encourage him to benefit from more exercise. He wrote a joky letter to Jaeger, professing to be a 'Professional Trick Bicyclist,' offering Mr. Phoebus as 'not a free wheel, but a free bike,' and suggesting that Jaeger might be inspired to compose some music on it. A further letter revealed the nature of Elgar's feelings about cycling, when he told Jaeger, 'I hope it will carry you as safely & as exhilaratingly as it has done me.' The offer was gratefully accepted, although the small-built and rather frail Jaeger seemed to find difficulties in becoming a successful and confident cyclist, despite Elgar's advice not to expect to achieve much at first, and not to give up under a month's hard work. Perhaps it was the same counsel he offered his wife Alice, whose own cycling had continued sporadically since the Birchwood days. What she described as 'a drefful bruisy fall' about this time seems to have ended her cycling career once and for all. Then there were problems with her husband's new Sunbeam, which in those days before assembly-line mass-production, did not finally arrive until the middle of March: 'E just starting for ride on his new bicycle. Alas! brake went wrong. Thank God no accident.'

The next day Mr. Robbins himself came and took the machine away for attention. After all, his advertisement had promised 'if you require your machine overhauled . . . I can give you satisfaction, and the price shall be right.' Despite its unpromising start the new machine looked impressive as Elgar posed with it for a photograph. Perhaps it was fitted with the new invention, the two-speed gear. It certainly seems to have had a newer design of brakes, for under his left hand is the lever for the 'hand-applied rear rim brake.' It featured also a type of oil-can which was stored in the seat tube below the saddle, avoiding the possibility of messy leaks. With its stirrup-rim front brake, mudguard flaps, bell, toolbag equipped with four extra-light spanners 'supplied gratis,' comfortable touring saddle and another oil-bath chain-case, the new machine was obviously finished to a very high standard of workmanship and must have been very much a gentleman's bicycle 'de luxe.' Soon Elgar was telling Jaeger, 'The new bike is friendly,' so Mr. Robbins' attentions must have done the trick.

A performance of *Gerontius* at Hanley intervened, after which Elgar fell victim to lumbago, so that it was early April before cycling was resumed, and then only for three or four outings to familiar places such as Upton, Pershore and Worcester. But there was one place in particular that was visited again that month, a place that, as Alice noted, was becoming more and more connected with work on *The Apostles* – Longdon Marsh, some seven miles south-east of Malvern: 'E finishing Judas scene, for a long ride after lunch the Marsh &c . . .' Billy Reed wrote:

> *Here he used to sit and dream. A great deal of* The Apostles *took shape in his mind there . . . he had to go there more than once to think out those climaxes in the Ascension; for they had to be built up each time that they never reached such a pitch of intensity as at the last and greatest climax, or he would have felt that the architecture of this movement was imperfect.*

Elgar also often visited the nearby Queenhill Church, where he was reduced on one occasion to tearing down the Births, Marriages and Deaths list from the wall of the porch in order to note down a sudden inspiration on the back of it. The full score of *The Apostles* would bear the inscription, 'In Longdon Marsh, 1902-3.' As Percy Young says in his *Elgar, O.M.*, the work has some claim to be the only oratorio produced as the result of cycling. As the music progressed, some further rides were undertaken with Dr. Grindrod, to Bushley, Bromsberrow and Kilcot, and perhaps both men were particularly keen to inspect one of the treasures of

Bromsberrow Church, a glass case containing two Civil War flags, belonging to two brothers who fought on opposing sides. Another joint expedition to Hasfield was spoilt when a storm came on. The two men waited at the Duke of York, hoping it would pass over, but eventually they were reduced to putting themselves and their bicycles on a passing baker's cart. Another misadventure was light-heartedly reported in a letter to Winifred Norbury's sister Florence, who had proposed calling on the Elgars:

I am to say we shall be delighted to see you on Friday – only I may be away biking . . . A man knocked me off in Upton on to the pavement – I was nearly killed – I wish I could say my last cry was "Florence!" – but it wasn't – it was a very wicked word.

May, June and July that year were very busy months. The orchestration of *The Apostles* was begun at the end of June, and continued through July, when Elgar spent a working holiday in Wales, taking his bicycle with him and using it to explore the area around Bettwys-Y-Coed. The score was eventually finished by the middle of August, and Elgar was free to enjoy some summer cycling, as he had after the completion of work on *Gerontius* three years before. Often an early riser, he wrote to Jaeger at this time, 'I went for ride 6 am this morning. Cold to the tummy!' With Dr. Grindrod he reached Tewkesbury, Eckington and Bredon, and then undertook a solo ride to Gloucester, although rain forced a return journey by train from Newent. Finally that month there was an ambitious two-day expedition with Grindrod to Ross and beyond, although the return was again by train. Alice was as always rather anxious about her husband, but she was the recipient of two reassuring telegrams, and all went well:

E started about 11 with Dr. Grindrod for the Forest. They rode to Ross & lunched then rode on to the Speech House, lovely day & beautiful ride. Had rooms at Speech House . . . good news from E twice thank God.

September saw Elgar cycling to Hereford once more for that year's Three Choirs Festival, and two days after his return a photographer from the *Daily Sketch* called at Craeg Lea and took fourteen shots of him, indoors and out, for an article in their series of 'Photographic Interviews.' It was eventually published in October, and included an impres-

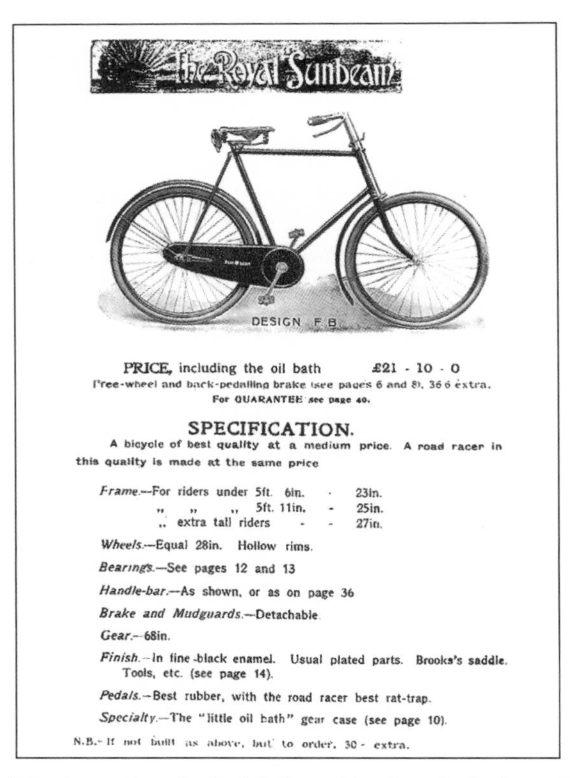

The Royal Sunbeam

DESIGN F.B.

PRICE, including the oil bath £21 - 10 - 0

Free-wheel and back-pedalling brake (see pages 6 and 8), 36/6 extra.

For GUARANTEE see page 40.

SPECIFICATION.

A bicycle of best quality at a medium price. A road racer in this quality is made at the same price

Frame.—For riders under 5ft. 6in. - 23in.
,, ,, ,, 5ft. 11in. - 25in.
,, extra tall riders - - 27in.

Wheels.—Equal 28in. Hollow rims.

Bearings.—See pages 12 and 13

Handle-bar.—As shown, or as on page 36

Brake and Mudguards.—Detachable.

Gear.—68in.

Finish.—In fine black enamel. Usual plated parts. Brooks's saddle. Tools, etc. (see page 14).

Pedals.—Best rubber, with the road racer best rat-trap.

Specialty.—The "little oil bath" gear case (see page 10).

N.B.—If not built as above, but to order, 30/- extra.

Details of Elgar's new free-wheel, oil-bath machine from the Sunbeam Catalogue. He bought such a model in 1903 and it seems to have lasted for the remaining six years of his cycling career. (And overleaf)

CARTER'S AND MARSTON'S

THE GEAR CASE.

This invention has made the Sunbeam the best cycle in the world for road riding, for—

1. The chain and chain wheels are actually rendered dustproof.

2. The chain and chain wheels lap through a little bath of oil, which removes all grind or friction.

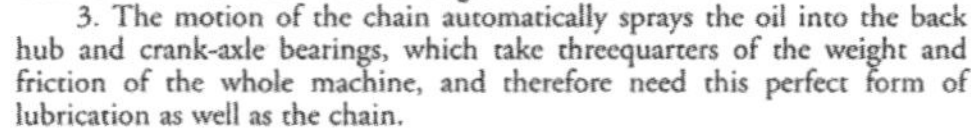

3. The motion of the chain automatically sprays the oil into the back hub and crank-axle bearings, which take threequarters of the weight and friction of the whole machine, and therefore need this perfect form of lubrication as well as the chain.

The Sunbeam Gear Case thus *diminishes* friction, and so *increases* speed. Further, by cleanliness and perfect lubrication, the parts of the cycle—the chain and chain wheels—that receive the *most* wear, suffer the *least;* in fact, under these conditions they have never been known to wear out.

The Oil for the bath is added to the case, or when dirty emptied out, at a screwed hole C. (See pages 22 and 23.)

A rattling in the case is merely a sign that the chain needs adjusting.

Chain Adjustment, which is rarely necessary, is effected by loosening nuts on either side marked A, and screwing up evenly the nuts marked B.

To Examine or Remove the Chain Wheels.—The above illustration shows how expeditiously this may be done; far sooner than with other pattern gear cases. The detachable disc should be levered out with a coin, and drawn over the crank. Customers are, however, advised that it is rarely necessary to open their chain cases.

Detachable Gear Cases are not fitted to Sunbeams on account of their liability to rattle and leak.

N.B.—The leather cover shown on page 34 is to protect a lady's dress from contact with the chain. It must not be confused with a gear case.

sive picture of Elgar posing by the gate with the new bicycle and Carice in the background, with the caption, 'Nothing like outdoor life.' But there was very little further 'outdoor life' that year as proof-correcting on *The Apostles* took over, followed by its first performance, a major event, in mid-October. It was a great success and Elgar's reputation stood even higher than before; so did his bank balance, for payment from Novello's for the new work had been generous, and the Elgars spent most of that winter in Italy.

They returned in February, 1904, and another orchestral masterpiece, the *In the South* Overture, inspired by sights and impressions of Italy, was finished on the twenty-first. It was ready for performance as part of a unique tribute to Elgar's genius, a three-day Festival of his music held at Covent Garden and attended by the cream of London society including the King and Queen. Elgar was most definitely 'arriving' and no doubt Alice continued to dream of a knighthood for her husband. The weather was frequently too poor for much cycling that spring, with winds, floods and snow. Elgar seems to have put his cycle clips on just three times in February, once in April and twice in May. Longdon was revisited but Elgar was unhappy with changes that had been made: 'E rode to Longdon Marsh, but found telegraph wires & clock face repainted &c. Very mis.'

Alice herself was very busy at this time, house-hunting, for she felt that a bigger residence would mark her husband's increasing fame and status, and stimulate more music. New building oppposite Craeg Lea was spoiling the view of the Severn Valley, and perhaps Malvern was becoming just a little too small and provincial for the newly grand composer. No doubt Elgar was happy to leave a town whose schools had seen him pass so many unhappy hours as a mere violin teacher. So Alice looked further afield, and in the end decided on a large detached house just outside Hereford, which Elgar named Plas Gwyn. It would be a centre from which Elgar would cycle to explore a whole new range of beautiful countryside.

That April, Elgar's collaborator on the *Coronation Ode*, A. C. Benson – the man who wrote the words of *Land of Hope and Glory* – was enjoying a cycling holiday in the Cotswolds with a friend. Basing themselves at the *Lygon Arms*, Broadway, the pair found their way to many of Elgar's own cycling haunts, including Evesham, Tewkesbury, Elmley Castle, Bredon, Pershore, Stratford and Worcester, with the Malvern Hills as a constant background. Benson's diary for the period contains many evocative descriptions of such places, in particular of Bredon and Elmley Castle, both places that Elgar himself had found while bicycling:

We had ginger-beer at a little shop, with affectionate careful people to serve us; and then pushed up Bredon by a pleasant wooded dingle. We were soon on the bare grass fields, and struggling up through what looked like an old earthwork. Then on a long nearly flat stretch of grass, to an old tower over Woollas Hall. The hill went down quite steeply in one place, with bluffs. Elmley Castle lay nestling below, with church and lake; and we had an incomparable view over leagues of pleasant plains, full of wood, and water, and green fields and hamlets. Bredon lies isolated from all other hills and is so central that we could see Gloucester in the South West, Tewkesbury, Pershore – and practically all the walks and rides we have taken. What a sweet and beautiful place, and how easy to live in the world looks when it lies at one's feet!

There were glints of water all over the plain – the Avon like a ribbon, the Severn like a sheet of steely blue. The hills loomed shadowy through the haze . . . We turned back and walked easily down; through a different dingle, where a bird sang sweetly, with the fragrant scent of the orchards below; and then through the orchards and past pretty nestling houses.

That excursion was the last of the holiday. Next day saw an unwilling departure, and a poetic farewell to Elgar country:

Then finished packing, tips etc. Sent off baggage and ourselves bicycled to Evesham. It was a strange day, with so thick a haze as to be almost a fog. We went down the pretty pleasant street, and I said 'Goodbye, Broadway!' as we passed the last house. I hated going from a place where I have had a time of nearly uninterrupted happiness and pleasure. The one very striking thing as we rode into Evesham was the bloom of the orchards. Since we last rode that way all the pear and plum orchards have burst into bloom; acres and acres are white with them. The hills, with trees in ordered rows, look like great fleeces – and the delicate fragrance filled the air.

The Elms, *the home of Elgar's sister Polly and her husband William, who was manager of a saltworks nearby.*
(A postcard photograph)

Elgar and his father photographed in the garden of The Elms, *Stoke Prior, near Bromsgrove, on 23 June 1904.*
Elgar had cycled over that day with the news of his Knighthood.

Benson had given up Alpine climbing after an accident, becoming determined to discover his own country instead. He was not the only literary cyclist, for along with Conan Doyle and Mark Twain, H. G. Wells, Bernard Shaw and Bertrand Russell – among many others – were devotees of the saddle. None of them went so far in praise of the bicycle as Benson, however, who penned an extra verse to St. Francis' Hymn to the Sun:

> Praised be thou, O my Lord, of our brother the *Bicycle*,
> Who holdeth his breath when he runneth,
> And is very swift and cheerful and unwearied, and silent.
> He beareth us hither and thither very patiently,
> And when he is sick he doth not complain.

For the Elgars, May saw another trip to Germany, and it was not until his return in early June that Elgar began some cycling that year. Faced with organising the house move, Alice was no doubt happy to have her husband out of the way, and Elgar several times biked from Craeg Lea to Hereford to show the new house off to fellow-cyclists such as Dora Penny and Rosa Burley. There was an interruption on 21 June, when he travelled to Durham University to receive another honorary degree, and next day, while he was returning to Malvern, a letter came for him from Arthur James Balfour, the Prime Minister. Mr. Balfour was musical, and he also shared an interest in cycling with Elgar, although his proficiency was not great; he had been known to appear on the Treasury Bench with an arm in a sling and a foot in a slipper. Some years earlier he had arrived at Hawarden by bicycle, to be greeted by a mildly shocked and bemused Mr. Gladstone, whom he considered to be 'peculiarly sensitive in the matter of dignities.' Alice must have guessed what the letter contained, and locked it away safely. She went to Great Malvern station to meet her husband, and they travelled on together to Malvern Wells. She told him of the letter from 10 Downing Street that was waiting at home. 'Has it come?' asked Elgar with a light in his face, but then went on to suppose it was about matters connected with copyright law – something that he was concerned with.

The letter proved to be the long-awaited offer of a knighthood. 'Both very pleased' wrote Alice. They seem to have kept the news to themselves for the rest of that day, but Elgar's last cycle rides from Craeg Lea before the move to Hereford were to visit family and friends to tell them personally of the honour. The next day, before anything else, he cycled over to Stoke Prior near Bromsgrove to tell his father, who was staying with Elgar's sister Polly and her family at their house, The Elms. His niece May took a historic photograph of father and son in the garden, Elgar in rather dusty cycling clothes standing almost diffidently behind the proud old man. The next day he bought a newspaper to see the official announcement of the honour, and rode to the Norburys to show them. Finally a few days later he 'wobbled round' to Birchwood House and enjoyed a celebratory lunch with Squire Little, his former bicycle teacher. No doubt there were some amusing reminiscences of those lessons to be shared, but I daresay the Squire would have been staggered had he known that his violin teacher friend would within some four years have become an internationally famous composer and a Knight of the Realm to boot.

The next day, 29 June, 1904, the move to Plas Gwyn took place, with Elgar pedalling most of the way. His Malvern cycling days were over, and it was time to say farewell to the many beautiful and atmospheric places he had found – Kempsey and Spetchley, Colwall and Cradley, Castlemorton and Bredon, Eastington and Longdon, all with their views of the Malvern Hills. He had woven them into the fabric of his music, but there were many new places to be found, and much new music, to come.

Intermezzo

'Dorabella'

Among Elgar's cycling lady friends, none, not even Rosa Burley, seemed quite so bold and determined a cyclist as Dora Penny, the daughter of the Rector and Rural Dean of Wolverhampton. Perhaps circumstances contributed to an independent outlook. Dora's mother had died shortly after giving birth, and she had been brought up by her grandmother while her father volunteered his services to the Melanesian Mission for twelve years. Not until 1895, the year of her twenty-first birthday, did Dora live with her father, on his appointment to Wolverhampton, and she had to make further adjustments when he married for a second time, to Mary Frances Baker of the Hasfield Court family. Earlier, Miss Baker had been a good friend of Alice Roberts, as she then was, of nearby Redmarley, and the friendship continued. Dora thus became one of the Elgar circle and she was instantly fascinated by him, enjoying his company as much and as frequently as she could, if only just within the bounds of Victorian propriety; on several occasions, for example, they went together to see Wolverhampton Wanderers play at home. More conventionally, Dora and her step-mother visited the Elgars at Malvern by train every so often. She invented a dance to the *Lullaby* from his *Scenes from the Bavarian Highlands* and under her nickname of Dorabella became the subject of a dance-like *Intermezzo* in the *Enigma* Variations which affectionately mimicked her stutter.

The meetings with Elgar were not frequent enough, perhaps, for Dora, and she must have realised that undertaking the journey to Malvern by bicycle, however unorthodox such a venture might seem, would provide independence of her step-mother, who was no doubt busy enough with the running of the Rectory. It was one tiny example of how the bicycle became a liberator for women, providing greater personal mobility. In his 1979 novel, *Elgar on the Journey to Hanley*, Keith Alldritt described the first of several solo cycle rides that Dora Penny made from Wolverhampton to see the Elgars – a journey of some forty miles – setting the girl's feelings within the social world of her times, and evoking the urban-industrial and rural landscape of Elgar's England:

'Very early one morning . . . Dora set off. She wore a straw hat and a linen jacket and skirt of subdued yellow colour. Her portmanteau and oilskin were strapped to the rear of her cycle. Not that she thought that she would need the oilskin, for the weather continued fine and hot. The sky over the blast furnaces and factory stacks was a brilliant blazing blue.

Turning left Dora pedalled slowly past the Old Mitre Inn, Pounds House *and the Prebend House. The bright early morning sun illuminated the ivy on the walls of these two elegant houses of the early eighteenth century. The town streets were not yet busy. Dora was excited at the thought of the day's adventure before her. She freewheeled across the central square and moved, ever more confidently, past the* Star and Garter Hotel *with its high narrow gables and the 'Victoria Drapery and Supply Stores' whose proprietor, Mr. James Beattie, was at this very moment supervising the lowering of sunblinds over the windows of his shop. He made a very formal bow to the Rector's daughter, who could only manage to remove a hand from the handlebars for one brief flick of a wave. The portly businessman gazed after her in some surprise.*

She gathered speed as she proceeded down the slope of this street past the shops and the fine old town houses. She came into a poorer quarter with many squalid-looking little taverns. Then she was going past the high factories built a century before. The clamour was upsetting, deafening to her. Factory hands lounging by the blackened Doric columns of the gate watched her curiously as she hastened past. Then she was among the cots of the nailers. Their dwellings and workshops, all of old maroon brick, stood at inexplicable angles under trees by little streams. And then as these buildings came to an end she found herself at last out in the clean quiet countryside among the gently glowing fields. She was on the high road to Worcester.

Dora was exhilarated. She pedalled away increasing her speed. She felt that she could go on like this for ever. She rejoiced in her freedom. She felt like singing.

She glided past large lurching wagons. Once she made the horses rear up. The older drivers turned and raised their hats to her, their respect mixed with puzzlement. The younger men regarded her more blatantly and cheekily. A girl on a cycle was no part of the forms and traditions of deference that they knew. Many had never seen a cyclist before.

She came into the green undulating landscape of Worcestershire. There came a fork in the narrow cobbled road that ran between the luxuriant hedgerows. The left would have taken her into Stourbridge with all its glass-blowing kilns. Dora remembered the Bishop telling her how the young Dr Johnson had walked there from Lichfield to visit his cousin Cornelius Ford. But she would go to the right down a narrow wooded highway that eventually brought her into Kidderminster. She cycled straight through the centre, past the town hall and the statue of Sir Rowland Hill. Here there were a few other lady cyclists moving slowly and demurely from shop to shop. They looked with wonder and respect after the now slightly dishevelled girl who was obviously a cyclist of great distances.

The air here was troubled with the deep rumble of the steam looms in the carpet factories. There was the heavy, incessant rhythm of thud and clank and hum, thud and clank and hum . . . She was relieved when she was beyond the town and back among the fields and pastures of the woods.

But now she was beginning to feel afraid. There was a tiredness in her feet and thighs that made them feel light and disjointed. Twice she had to stop and sit on a milestone to restore herself. She looked with some dismay on the decreasing but still considerable number of miles yet to cover. In all, her journey to Malvern would amount to more than forty miles.

The day was now hot and Dora perspired heavily at her brow, her waist and under her arms. A fear that she had attempted more than she could achieve grew upon her. With legs quivering she pedalled slowly into the village of Ombersley. It was a handsome place, its main street composed almost entirely of black and white buildings. It was like entering the past.

The King's Arms *was a large inn with three gables of half-timbering. It was of Queen Elizabeth's time or even earlier. It had two low wooden doors that opened straight on to the village street. A stout figure of a man in a smock lounging by the casement took off his cap as Dora approached.*

'Good day to you, miss.' For all his sleepily slothful calm he was astounded to see this beautiful fair-haired girl come pedalling through Ombersley. He studied her most carefully. He had never seen a bicycle before, though he had heard of the invention. It had never occurred to him that a woman, a lady, might ride one.

'Good day.' Dora tried to summon the proper pleasantness.

'Bit 'ot, eh?' He motioned with his hand at the warm, deserted village street.

'Yes, it is rather.'

'Might I invite you to step inside and have a drink? We've ale, small beer, cordial, wine . . . dandelion and burdock, if you like . . .'

He had a kind red face. He was courteous and fatherly. Shakily Dora dropped a foot to the ground and stopped and considered. Her legs trembled visibly. The man's voice had a strong Worcestershire burr. She was far from Wolverhampton now. And she felt so very weary. But for a lady to go into a public house alone!

'I have brought some sandwiches. Might I eat th . . . th . . . them inside?'

'Of course you might, if that is your desire. Please to get down and come inside and rest yourself from the sun.'

Stiffly Dora dropped from the Dursley-Pedersen which the man took from her. He studied it with the closest interest as he carried it down the two steps that led to the front room of the inn. He was a stout, well-fed man and could have been a farmer as well as an innkeeper.

Inside it was dark and cool. There were ancient benches and settles around the walls and the low plaster ceiling was of the time of King James I, with mouldings of a rose and a mermaid.

'I'll just fetch my wife,' said the landlord with a simple kindly delicacy. He added, 'And what should you like to drink ?'

'I should like to have some of the dandelion and burdock, if you please,' replied Dora.

The man's footsteps could be heard slowly descending stone steps. Dora sat back and rested. How she savoured the quiet gloom and coolness of this room!

The man returned with a stone bottle of dandelion and burdock in his hand. He was followed by his wife, a thin, bony-faced woman in a dark dress who hung back, surveying Dora, like one who came to see a wonder.

The innkeeper poured the drink into a pewter tankard and Dora drank it up. It was profoundly and delicately cool to her mouth. It was an ecstasy to drink it. She could not recall drinking anything in her life before that refreshed her as this did. It was a restorative that drove all the heat and weariness out of her.

The inkeeper's wife watched Dora's every movement. The sudden appearance in the village of this handsome girl in her suit of such an elegant shade of yellow was to this countrywoman like something out of a fairy tale.

'And how far have you come, miss?' she enquired after a while, her curiosity overcoming both her diffidence and her sense of the respect due to a lady.

When Dora told her, the woman gasped, opening her toothless mouth and turning to her husband in surprise and alarm.

'And 'ow far be ye goin'?'

The reply produced similar expressions of shock. The girl and her shiny bicycle were almost unbelievable.

Dora enjoyed the admiration that accompanied their surprise and their anxiety.

Her confidence and her energy were becoming restored.

When the time came to set off again, she mounted her cycle with enthusiasm. She felt much encouraged by the friendly deferential farewells of the two older people.

Off she went, back into the rolling green countryside. She rode a little more slowly now. But she was calm and content. For much of the way the only sound was the distant hum of bees. She pedalled away with a sense of happiness, achievement and freedom. Twenty years on . . . she would remember the pleasure of her first journey to Malvern on that warm bright summer day when Lord Salisbury was still Prime Minister and the old Queen still reigned.

Dora was much reassured when she saw the tower of Worcester cathedral appear in the distance. As she pedalled slowly through the streets of the county town she was struck by how much elegance there was here compared with Wolverhampton. There were ladies in French hats in the Foregate, glossy prosperous clergymen in the area near the cathedral and many a handsome horse and carriage that she had to negotiate her way past with care.

She crossed the bridge over the Severn with another thrill of excitement. This was one more proud occasion in her career as a lone traveller. . . This excitement sustained her as she moved on into the countryside again down the narrow bumpy road that led to Powick. But as she moved past the large church in that village her legs were beginning to ache again in a disconcertingly shivering way. She encouraged herself with the thought that she was now close to her destination. And in less than an hour she could see the harsh red brick of the villas standing up from the rich green of the surrounding fields. North Hill was large and hazy in the heavy warm air of the late afternoon.

. . . She had done the forty miles! She dropped from her bicycle with a feeling of relief and pride. Her skirt stuck to her bottom and her face was soiled with black lines of perspiration. For all the fairness of her colouring, there was now a certain swarthiness to Dora's appearance, somewhat like that of a gypsy. She tried, without much success, to tidy her hair before passing through the garden gate.'

Alldritt errs in assigning a Dursley-Pedersen machine to Dora, for she lived in Wolverhampton, and knew and visited John Marston's bicycle factory. She owned a Sunbeam, in fact, and Elgar's adoption of this make may have been at her persuasion. Like Elgar, Dora was fascinated by gadgetry and bought a cyclometer from the Army & Navy Stores, enabling her to record a total of three hundred and ninety-eight and a half miles after a cycling holiday in 1899.

Her solo journeys to Malvern around the turn of the century say much for her courage, and presumably indicate too, something of a tolerant attitude at the Rectory. Cycling was very much a symbol of the widely discussed phenomenon of the emancipated 'new woman' of the mid nineties, a phenomenon vehemently opposed in some quarters. For a long time no 'nice' women rode bicycles, wrote Ethel Smyth, predictably enough a keen cyclist herself as early as 1890. The writer Eliza Lynn Linton frequently denounced the lady cyclist in her articles for various women's magazines, for she was bound to be the kind of person who despised her home and womanly work, disobeyed her parents, smoked cigarettes, and read risky novels. On one occasion she wrote that the lady cyclist had not 'the faintest remnant of that sweet spirit of allurement which, conscious or unconscious, is woman's supreme attraction,' and on another she defined the real anxiety lurking at the back of her mind, 'This modern bicycling craze is not only far beyond a girl's strength,' she wrote, 'but it tends to destroy the sweet simplicity of her girlish nature. Besides, how dreadful it would be if by some accident she were to fall off into the arms of a strange man!'

There was help at hand to guard against such a fate. An announcement in *The Queen, The Lady's Newspaper* for 16 May 1896, informed an anxious readership of the formation of the Chaperon Cyclists' Association, 'to provide gentlewomen of good social position to conduct ladies on bicycle excursions and tours . . . many ladies have a great objection to their daughters cycling without a proper and efficient escort . . . excursions by the day or for longer periods might be made in the country by young ladies having a chaperon with them, which could not be attempted without.' The complete respectability of the organisation was guaranteed by the standards it set for its employees. 'Those desirous of becoming chaperons as members of the association must be either married ladies, widows, or unmarried ladies over thirty years of age. They must furnish three references, two to ladies of undoubted social position, and one to a clergyman of the Church of England, or to a justice of the peace.'

A rather less formal picture of the Eternal Feminine on wheels may be glimpsed from a letter of another keen cyclist, Thomas Hardy. 'I asked an omnibus conductor if the young women (who ride recklessly into the midst of the traffic) did not meet with accidents. He said, "Oh nao; their sex pertects them. We dares not drive over them, wotever they do; and they do jist wot they likes."'

Hereford Days

'Heavenly country to ride in...'

Barely a week after that cycle ride to *Plas Gwyn*, Elgar faced the pomp and circumstance of being knighted by the King at Buckingham Palace – a memorable occasion indeed for the piano-tuner's son. But the very next day the new grandee was back at Hereford and back in the humble saddle, riding to Brockhampton, no doubt making sure to see the famous timbered manor house, with his niece May, who had come to live with the Elgars as companion and help. She was to be a frequent cycling partner, as was the fourteen-year old Carice after some lessons. That first month Elgar set a new Sunday pattern by cycling the short distance to Belmont Abbey for Mass, and made other rides either with May or the eccentric Hereford organist George Robertson Sinclair, finding villages like Woolhope, Fownhope and Kilpeck. There was an interruption when he had to adjudicate at the Morecambe Festival, created by his friend Canon Gorton, and Elgar's cycling days at Plas Gwyn were to be more and more disrupted as the demands of growing fame took him away from home with increased frequency. He was in London during August, and biked just four times that month, including a ride with Dora Penny to Holme Lacy to see some small car trials. Cars were becoming a sign of the times. Ironically enough, the technology which had been developed to improve the bicycle went on to play its part in the emergence of both motor-cycles and motor-cars, and the Sunbeam firm was one of several that went on to produce the new vehicles.

There were several outings in September after the Gloucester Three Choirs, with Canon Gorton and with Rosa Burley who came over from Malvern to stay. Alice noted that they found Hoarwithy and Fawley that month, and that there was some good cycling weather. At the beginning of October there was the Leeds Festival, and then Elgar's friend the retired banker, Frank Schuster, came to stay. He arrived in his Fiat motor, complete with chauffeur, and two or three days of four-wheeled touring began, to Symonds Yat and Monmouth, and back to Malvern to see old friends like Troyte Griffith, Lady Mary Lygon and the Norburys. Alice was delighted with the easy, quick pace of such travelling, and she loved the country views as much as her husband. Motor touring made up for her lack of success as a cyclist and there would be more and more expeditions in cars hired for the day during the Hereford years. Elgar and May went out riding just three times that October, including a trip to Checkley and Backbury Beacon, where Alice and Carice met them having come by pony and trap; and cycling concluded that year with just two rides in November. One of them was to Ledbury, where they had lunch with Troyte Griffith. An enthusiastic cyclist, he undertook the ride from Malvern to Hereford to see the Elgars on many occasions. Composing seems to have slackened off amid the excitement of the knighthood and the house move, but in November Elgar finished another *Pomp & Circumstance* March. The first discussions about the creation of a special Professorship of Music at Birmingham University for him also took place, and Elgar ultimately accepted the post although it would mean many unhappy hours indoors preparing lectures.

1905 was to prove a busy year almost from the start of the cycling season. Elgar and May got out for a tentative ride as early as 3rd February, but work on the *Introduction and Allegro for Strings* supervened. Not only is this an exhilarating fresh-air piece if ever there was one, full of that 'outdoor kind of spirit,' but its three-part structure seems to suggest the pattern of a journey, a cycle tour in music – the setting out, the arrival at a destination, and the joyful return home. Then there was another official engagement in the form of an honorary degree at Oxford, and the Elgars took opportunity to spend a few days in the City seeing the sights and paying a call on Richard Baxter Townshend. Perhaps he characteristically insisted on showing Elgar the tricycle, and went on to give a demonstration. But Elgar seems to have remained content with two wheels. The string piece was finished halfway through February, and then were were proofs of the March to deal with, but time was found for expeditions to Worcester and Marcle, despite strong winds. Of the Marcle trip, Alice's diary comment shows how determined her husband was to avoid indoor commitments and enjoy some fresh air: 'E did not go to W. Philc meeting or Worcester Historical but for long ride with May.'

The pace of life quickened, with an invitation to visit America in the summer to be dealt with, and more proof-correcting. London rehearsals for the first performances of the *Introduction and Allegro for Strings* and the March had to be attended, and the first lecture of Elgar's controversial Birmingham Professorship followed hard on the heels of the premières. It was a frantically busy period and the strain left Elgar feeling unwell. There was just one cycle ride in March.

April seemed more conducive, and Alice recorded no less than ten outings, although she was, unusually, not very specific about the destinations, often merely noting 'long day out.' Weobley, a pretty town with a remarkable 14th century church tower, was however mentioned as a new discovery. Towards the end of the month Troyte Griffith rode over to stay. Once again Alice did not always record where they went, but Griffith himself left an amusing vignette of a search for an old building. With his architectural and artistic interests, the idea for such an expedition probably came from Griffith himself. He remembered:

> *We bicycled out from Hereford to see a 14th century building attached to a farm house. When we came out the daughter of the house asked us to come in for tea. Rather to my surprise Elgar accepted the invitation. After tea he offered a cigarette to our hostess with the words 'I know you smoke.' When we got outside I said to him 'You have never seen that girl before why did you say you knew she smoked?' 'That's all you know about it,' said Elgar. 'She was at Miss – 's school at Malvern and all the girls there smoked.'*

Plus ça change . . . After Troyte's return to Malvern there were just half a dozen rides during May, including a venture with a friend part of the way to Ludlow. Griffith came again at the end of the month and together they found Abbey Dore, whose church of St. Mary, the survivor of a 12th century Cistercian foundation, contains two late 13th century effigies of mail-clad knights. They would be certain to attract Elgar, with his love of the age of chivalry and heraldry. But it was the last ride for many weeks, until Elgar's return from America in the middle of July. On the 22nd he attempted what Alice described as 'a little ride,' and next day went for a jaunt with May after Mass at Belmont. It might have helped the muscles to tone up ready for an expedition with GRS of the Variations – who as an organist was renowned for another kind of pedalling – all the way to Ludlow a few days later, although matters were made easier by putting the machines on the train as far as Leominster. It was apparently a lovely day, and the two musicians enjoyed seeing the historic Castle. But there were times when Elgar found Sinclair an impossible cycling partner. After one of their joint expeditions he told Billy Reed:

> *You know, Sinclair is a funny person: he is a dear and I am very fond of him; but his ideas of companionship and mine differ materially. Yesterday he came up here and said, 'What a great day! I am going to persuade you to leave work for a little while, and come out cycling with me. We will go up over the hills and round through this place and that, and so on; and it won't be too tiring for you.' The words were hardly out of his mouth when he pedalled off at full speed, and I followed as fast as I could, just keeping him in view for some miles until we came to a steep hill. At the top he got off his machine and waited for me, just drinking in the view. I was pretty nearly done, and was looking forward to a rest. But the moment I came up to him he said, 'Isn't the view from here magnificent? But we mustn't stop too long to admire it: we must push on.' And up and off he went, coasting away down the other side of the hill like an avalanche. And he did that every time. At the top of every hill he would dismount and wait until I came up panting; but the moment I was within speaking distance he would expatiate upon the beauty of the spot until I was close up. Then he would warn me again that we mustn't stop: we must push on – and so ride away furiously.*
> *This went on until I saw him dismount outside my own gate and wait for me to catch up with him for the last time, thank heaven! 'Grand ride we have had together,' he shouted as soon as I was within earshot. 'I have enjoyed being with you' – and off he went to his own home. As a matter of fact, I had scarcely been near him, had never ridden a yard by his side; but he enjoyed it. Sinclair is a funny fellow.*

But Elgar was greatly shocked when Sinclair died suddenly in his fifties in 1917. At the last Three Choirs Festival he attended, at Hereford Cathedral in 1933, Elgar, chatting with various old friends one day, pointed out the Sinclair head carved over one of the doors and reminded Ivor Atkins of the bicycle rides all three had enjoyed together.

Market House and Barrett Browning Institute, Ledbury.
(Period postcard photograph)

On the last day of July there was a more companionable ride with May to Eardisland, another typically pretty black-and-white Herefordshire village with various notable old houses in addition to its church, and Weobley, and at the beginning of August Ivor Atkins biked over from Worcester to work with Elgar on the orchestration of his *Hymn of Faith*. On his return next day, Elgar and May – nicknamed 'Eeks' – rode part of the way back with him, with a minor adventure as related in a letter to Carice:

> *May & I escorted Mr Atkins to Withington & then went for a further ride: we 'struck' a bull in a field & he did not like us, or rather our bicycles which we were wheeling through the field: I made, for once, no suggestion as to 'waking him up' – he didn't want it. He woke us up & we fled! Then a man came with a stake out of a hedge & kept him at bay while Eeks & I discreetly withdrew. I have no words for bulls! beyond 'teeth' &c.*

The rest of the month saw Elgar making various outings, twice to Woolhope and on one occasion to Callow. Dr Grindrod came over from Malvern for a joint outing, but one Sunday when Elgar found a punctured tyre just as he was setting out for Belmont Abbey, Alice found him 'not at all up to walk.' It would have been the last ride before mid-October, for various diversions now came along. An American friend, Professor Sanford of Yale University, came to stay, and there were motor drives to show him the sights; then there was the regular September fixture of the Three Choirs Festival, this time at Worcester. It was a memorable occasion for Elgar because during it he was awarded the Freedom of the City, and at this heady time he accepted an invitation from his friend Admiral Lord Charles Beresford to take a month's cruise with the Mediterranean Fleet. On his return there were just two more cycle rides that year, including one to Fownhope, a short distance to the south-west of Hereford, before the winter took over, and with it a conducting tour, more Birmingham lectures and work on *The Kingdom*, the next big choral work. Life was getting very busy indeed, and Elgar was going to spend less and less time in the saddle.

With the pressure of another major work to be ready for the autumn, another time-consuming but lucrative American trip in the spring, more visits from friends who required entertaining, and bouts of poor health and depression, 1906 was a difficult year for

Eardisland
(Period postcard photograph)

Elgar and cycling seems to have been reduced to a minimum. He tried a ride with May towards the end of January, but the roads were too muddy, and a car was hired the next day to make up for the missed outing. There were just three rides out with May in February, and after one of them Alice wrote how her overworked husband was 'much better for being out.' His mood improved following discussions with Novello's, who agreed to accept a scaled-down version of his original plan for *The Kingdom*. It was a great weight off Elgar's mind and progress on the work improved. Frank Schuster came again and there were more motor drives amid continued composing, leaving time for just two cycle rides in March. Once again Alice noted the value of the exercise for her stressed husband: 'E & May rode to Belmont – long round home – out again after lunch lovely ride . . . E so enjoyed being out & looked so refreshed.'

The other ride that month was to Weston Beggard, which boasts a 13th century church and an octagonal 18th century dovecote at a nearby farm. April saw four outings, with a variety of partners including Griffith, Sinclair and Atkins, taking in such places as Fownhope, Lugwardine and Brinsop, whose 14th century church of St George is noted for its sculpture, paintings and stained glass. The last ride was with Atkins on 5 April, and the very next day saw the Elgars leaving for the States, to return at the end of May. There was hardly any cycling until much later in the year, and not a great deal then. Amid the final preparations and rehearsals for *The Kingdom* première, Elgar made one outing with May in August, two in September, and two in October. His last ride of the year, strangely enough, was to previous haunts like Longdon Marsh and nearby Ham Court, putting his bike on the train to Malvern to make the trip more manageable. The atmsophere of the Marsh seemed to fascinate him still, and Elgar may have wished he was back in the Malvern days when he was able to do so much more cycling.

More time was spent in Italy that winter, and when Elgar returned towards the end of February 1907, he was at home for just two or three days before setting off for another American journey from which he returned at the end of April. Carice had been having cycling lessons, and almost immediately her proud father began to take her out with him. The month of May finally saw cycling taken up consistently again, with various outings with Carice, May, or Troyte Griffith. The rolling Herefordshire countryside began to be more systematically explored, with new places being noted in Alice's diary, including Pembridge, Dinmore – originally a preceptory of the Knights of St John of Jerusalem – and Eardisly, where the church of St May Magdalene has a famous Norman font, and where there is a Motte and Bailey Castle mentioned in Domesday. Elgar seemed keen to make up for his neglect of cycling, and once again it went hand in hand with music, as he went back to pieces he had composed as a child for a family play, and rearranged them into proper orchestral form as the *Wand of Youth* Suites. He was approaching his fiftieth birthday and wrote to Jaeger:

> *We are enjoying the summer when the weather will let us: some days hot & then cold as is today. There is really no news: all goes steadily on: I shall be fifty next week they tell me, but I don't know it: I have my pipe & the bicycle & a heavenly country to ride in – so an end. I take no interest whatever in music now & just 'edit' a few old boyish manuscripts . . .*

The expeditions continued throughout June, to Ullinswick, Hampton Bishop, Burghill – with its Victorian County Lunatic Asylum – and Hoarwithy. But on the 8th Elgar mounted the saddle for a major undertaking: 'E started bicycling, perhaps towards London started about 11.30. Heard from about 4.30 safe at Evesham after lovely ride.'

Alice waited all the next day without news, but on the 10th the intrepid cyclist had arrived at Stratford on Avon, where wind and storms forced him to abandon the London attempt, at any rate by bicycle; the train came to the rescue again, and Alice met up with him at Paddington. The comforts of the Langham Hotel must have soothed some aching muscles, but Elgar evidently felt fit for many more rides that summer. During that month Alice heard the 'great beautiful tune' that was to become the basis of the First Symphony, and cycling and composing continued to thrive together as work progressed on the *Wand of Youth* music and the fourth *Pomp & Circumstance* March. July saw him riding to Withington, Holme Lacy and Ross to the south-east of Hereford, and then a long way in another direction over the Welsh border to Abergavenny. Elgar was covering impressive distances, and there was also a three-day expedition to his sister at Stoke Prior beginning on the 9th. 'E started with bag on bicycle about 11.15,' wrote Alice, having no doubt made sure that the maid had provided some extra-special sandwiches for her adored husband. Heavy rain forced him to take the train from Cleobury Mortimer, as he informed an anxious Alice by telegram, but the return journey through Great Witley and Bromyard was uneventful. A few days later, Elgar confessed to Alice that during an after-lunch ride by Holme Lacy it was 'so hot he lay by road side & slept', just like his hero Falstaff might have done, although we may confide the hope that on this occasion there was no snoring. Hopefully too, he was not accosted by the police on suspicion of vagrancy, like Gustav Mahler during one of his own cycling expeditions. Mahler, another keen cyclist, had undertaken a four-day tour amid the stunning scenery of the Ampezzo Valley during one of his summer breaks. Away from the formality of the Vienna Opera House, he donned an open-neck shirt and was grateful to abandon jacket, belt and braces. Some stubble appeared on the usually clean-shaven composer's face, and the tramp-like impression was complete. But the brush with the law did not seem to discourage him from riding and when Mahler later bought a new bicycle in Vienna he wrote to his wife Alma about it in words that Elgar and his friends would have recognised – 'I'm coming the day after tomorrow, early on Thursday . . . wobbling along on the bike.'

The Holme Lacy ride was virtually the end of cycling that year, as fishing seemed to take over in August, and there were periods away in Wales and at Ridgehurst. The new March was premièred in London at the beginning of September, and after the Gloucester Three Choirs, Alice recorded just one final ride on 18 September. There was more work on the Symphony and a projected Violin Concerto, and early in November the Elgars left for Italy once more and did not return to Hereford until the end of May 1908.

Cycling seems to have been one of Elgar's first thoughts on resuming life at Plas Gwyn, but the period of absence seems to have made the rapid development of motor transport all the more evident: 'E depressed about bicycling on account of motors . . .' wrote Alice on 1st June. But three days later there was a cycling threesome amid lovely weather. With Carice and May, Elgar found Wigmore Castle, another Domesday relic, Aymestry with its Iron Age Hill Fort, and Shobdon. The latter boasted Shobdon Arches, built around the Norman chancel arch, doorways and tympana of the old church, with pinnacles and battlements added. Elgar described it to Alice as a perfect expedition, but it may have been prompted by a mundane and rather noisy household chore: 'E & C & May out for bicycling day to escape vacuum cleaner.'

Elgar was understandably annoyed by unwelcome noises, and there had been a previous problem at Plas Gwyn over a neighbour's parrot. Work on the Symphony continued that month, and there was another visit from Dora Penny, who again cycled all the way from Wolverhampton; after a few days the indefatigable girl pedalled off again, all the way to Gloucester. From there she probably cycled all the way back home to Wolverhampton, a fifty-six mile journey she had already made two years previously. The weather was evidently proving an encouragement to cycling. In her diary for 30th June, Alice memorably evoked the atmosphere of a midsummer evening: 'Lovely day E for lovely ride late. He thought he had never felt or seen such lovely atmosphere in country & sights. Warm & still. Lovely roses.'

The previous day she had described him as being 'possessed' with the Symphony and Elgar's mind was no doubt geared up to a pitch of receptivity for the sights and scents of a beautiful evening. Two weeks later there was another, entirely different example of mental energy as he perpetrated one of his most excruciating word-plays during an outing with the girls. He explained it in a letter to Troyte Griffith.

> *Both the children are feeling unwell: riding yesterday I asked them if we should take tea in the Village of 'Synagoguinetta.' They professed ignorance of such village; I explained it was 'Little Dewchurch.' They nearly fell off their cycles & have felt mentally incapable ever since.*

There were fewer rides that August as work on the Symphony continued amid house guests and concerts in London and Belgium; one notable excursion was noted by Alice, a long excursion with May to the intriguingly named Hole in the Wall, followed by tea at Ross. There were some more rides in September, after the Worcester Three Choirs, as Elgar sought a change from the long hours he was working to complete the huge score of the Symphony. One outing was spoilt by a puncture and subsequent two-hour wait at Fawley station, and

Kilpeck Church near Hereford.
(Period postcard photograph)

another long expedition to the partly 14th century Winsley Hall was described by Alice as being 'with much walking.' She effectively evoked the undulating Herefordshire terrain when she also found her husband 'quite tired and rather sea-sick – such ascents and descents.' Perhaps the years were beginning to tell, but at any rate there was one more ride on the 25th, the day he put the last note to the score of the Symphony. Then there was a spell in London to correct proofs ready for the triumphant première of the work in December, and just three more cycle rides in October, with Troyte Griffith who came to stay. On the day of the last ride, Alice noted how her husband rested after lunch, and then went to Queen Anne's Mansions by train. It was the first mention of this flat in London, and being in Town was becoming more and more convenient and important for both the Elgars. They took various flats there over the next few years, and finally moved to Hampstead at the beginning of 1912.

1909 was virtually Elgar's last year of cycling. He was unwell and depressed early in January and took a cure at Llandridnod Wells. He occupied himself with a new indoor hobby, chemistry, and a resumption of kite-flying in March and April seemed to satisfy as far as fresh air and exercise was concerned. There was a holiday in Florence from April to June, and it was the beginning of July before cycling was thought of. Once again composition and biking were connected: 'E getting ready for cycle excursions & looking up sketches.'

But there were to be only some half dozen rides that month and four in August, including expeditions with either Troyte Griffith or Carice to Stoke, Ullingswick and Breinton. Later in August he worked on the Violin Concerto, and it is not difficult to feel the rolling landscape of Herefordshire and the Welsh Border in the rich textures of that work. The Concerto was not finished until June 1910, and it was on the sixth of that month that Elgar took his one and only cycle ride of that year, if Alice's diary is accurate. It may have been his last ride of all, nearly ten years since he took those lessons with Squire Little running alongside him through the narrow twisty lanes at Birchwood. The Elgars took the decision to leave *Plas Gwyn* and settle in London in a grand house in Hampstead, and the composer was to a certain extent cut off from the countryside and landscape that meant so much to him. There were frequent return visits, but not until

Old Brockhampton Manor
(Period postcard photograph)

nearly the end of the First World War was Elgar to take up country life again, when he spent periods at an isolated cottage, Brinkwells, near Fittleworth in the Sussex woods. The stimulus to composition was almost immediate, with the appearance of the 'Cello Concerto and the Chamber works. By then his cycling days were well and truly over, but Carice had kept her machine and often put it on the train from London to visit her parents and cycle round the village. No doubt she missed her father's company on the road, and some of those awful puns.

Still today, Elgar's much used cycling maps, one for Worcestershire and the other for Herefordshire, can be seen at the Birthplace Museum at Broadheath, near Worcester. They show the enormous distances his cycling expeditions covered, and a characteristically keen knowledge of his countryside environment. County boundaries were marked, and the various rivers, the Severn, the Teme, the Wye and the Lugg, were coloured in blue. He traced over all the roads he had cycled along in red, and as a result the Hereford map in particular is a mass of criss-crossing red lines, representing some thousands of miles. The lines seem to show that he tried to avoid going to the same place by the same route, and that return journeys were deliberately made along different roads from the outward journey. If so, it would be entirely characteristic of a man gifted with such a creative mind, always seeking fresh alternatives, always looking for the new amid the familiar, as a composer does.

Alice Elgar, as so often, summed matters up best when she wrote in her diary about one of those last rides from Plas Gwyn in the July of 1909: 'E for ride later. Loving the country & scenery.'

***

After many a dusty mile,
Wanderer, linger here awhile.
Stretch your limbs in this long grass;
Through these pines a wind shall pass
That shall cool you with its wing.

Grasshoppers shall shout and sing,
While the shepherd on the hill,
Near a fountain warbling still,
Modulates, when noon is mute,
Summer songs along his flute.

Underneath a spreading tree,
None so easy-limbed as he,
Sheltered from the dog-star's heat.

Rest; and then, on freshened feet,
You shall pass the forest through.
It is Pan that counsels you.

From the *Greek Anthology*, set by Elgar in 1902

Appendix

ELGAR'S DESTINATIONS

FROM MALVERN :

Berrow Green
Birchwood
Birtsmorton
Bosbury
Bredon
Broadwas
Bromsberrow
Bromyard
Bushley
Castlemorton,
Cilfton-upon-Teme
Colwall
Cradley
Dunston Castle
Eastington
Eckington
Evesham
Fernhill
Ham Court
Hanley Castle
Hasfield
Haw Bridge
Hawkhurst
Hereford
Kemerton
Kempsey
Kilcot
Knightsbridge
Leigh Sinton
Little Malvern
Longdon Marsh
Madresfield
Malvern Link
Malvern Wells Golf
Club
Much Cowarne
Newent
Pendock
Pershore
Ragged Stone
Redmarley Ridgeway
Ross
Rhydd
Shelsley Walsh
Southstone Rock
Spetchley
Stoke
Strensham
Stretton Grandison
Suckley
Tewkesbury
Upton

FROM HEREFORD:

Abbey Dore
Abergavenny
Belmont Abbey
Blackbury Beacon
Bosbury
Breinton
Brockhampton
Bromyard
Broxton
Burghill
Callow
Checkley
Cleobury Mortimer
Dinmore
Eardisly
Evesham
Fawley
Fownhope
Great Witley
Hampton Bishop
Hoarwithy
Holme Lacy
Kilpeck
Leominster
Little Dewchurch
Ludlow
Lugwardine
Marcle
Mordiford
Moorhampton
Peterchurch
Rembridge
Ross
Stoke
Stratford on Avon
Ullingswick
Weobley
Weston Beggard
Wigmore Castle
Withington
Woolhope
Worsley Hall

It would need another publication to do proper justice to the purely geographical aspect of Elgar's cycle explorations. All the places I have noted above can be easily found on current Ordnance Survey and motoring maps, and many atmospheric Elgarian haunts wait to be visited by those who wish to follow in his tracks. I hope the reader will find this useful in tracing the Churches, villages and pubs that Elgar cycled to, and in revealing the great range of his travels in the saddle.
